SHOW ME HOW TO
SHARE CHRIST IN
THE WORKPLACE

Show Me How Series

Show Me How to Share the Gospel
Show Me How to Answer Tough Questions
Show Me How to Illustrate Evangelistic Sermons
Show Me How to Preach Evangelistic Sermons

Other Books by R. Larry Moyer

21 Things God Never Said
31 Days to Contagious Living
31 Days to Living as a New Believer
31 Days to Walking with God in the Workplace
31 Days with the Master Fisherman
Free and Clear
Growing in the Family
Welcome to the Family

SHOW ME HOW

SHOW ME HOW TO
SHARE CHRIST IN
THE WORKPLACE

R. LARRY MOYER

Kregel
Publications

Published by Kregel Publications, a division of Kregel, Inc., P.O. Box 2607, Grand Rapids, MI 49501.

Library of Congress Cataloging-in-Publication Data
Moyer, R. Larry (Richard Larry), 1947–
 Show me how to share Christ in the workplace / R. Larry Moyer.
    p.   cm.—(Show me how series)
Includes bibliographical references.
1. Employees—Religious life. 2. Witness bearing (Christianity)
I. Title.
BV4593.M695   2012   248'.5—dc23   2012017314

ISBN 978-0-8254-4269-8

Printed in the United States of America
12 13 14 15 16 / 5 4 3 2 1

*To those in the workplace who see
their jobs as a calling and want to use
them to influence non-Christians*

Contents

Introduction

Welcome to Your Ministry

Two kinds of Christians go to work. One says, "I'm a Christian called to serve the Lord as a computer technician." The other says, "I'm a computer technician who happens to be a Christian." The first sees the workplace as his calling, and the second sees his faith and his work as coincidental. For the first person, his workplace is his ministry. For the second, his workplace is nothing more than a job.

Every committed Christian needs to recognize that he or she is in full-time ministry. The concept that professional, paid Christian workers such as pastors, associate pastors, music directors, and youth workers are the only ones in ministry could not be further from the truth. Exodus 31:1–3 says: "Then the LORD spoke to Moses, saying: 'See, I have called by name Bezalel the son of Uri, the son of Hur, of the tribe of Judah. And I have filled him with the Spirit of God, in wisdom, in understanding, in knowledge, and in all manner of workmanship.'" Bezalel was a craftsman, not a preacher, who was filled with the Spirit of God. God recognized his ability and chose him to be the principal workman in the construction of the tabernacle. Each day, as Bezalel worked with metal, wood, and stone, he was also deeply committed to God. Bezalel was in full-time ministry.

CEOs who live for Christ in their leadership positions, CPAs who live out their faith within the firm, nurses who see the hospital as a place of service, plumbers who see Christ as their employer—all are in full-time ministry. Just because they have not always been viewed as such does not change the truth. Author, radio speaker, and seminary professor Haddon Robinson once said, "If I were pastor of a church, I would ordain people to the workplace."[1]

When asked, "Which is the great commandment?" Jesus replied, "'You shall love the Lord your God with all your heart, with all your soul, and with all your mind.' This is the first and great commandment. And the second is like it: 'You shall love your neighbor as yourself'" (Matt. 22:37–39). Loving our neighbors or co-workers through service for Christ is as spiritual as going to church. Therefore, any Christian committed to serving the Savior where he or she labors—being used of God to the fullest extent possible—is in full-time ministry. To not see ourselves as such is sadly shortsighted.

Please don't misunderstand—I am fully aware that your employer is paying you to work, not witness. In Titus 2:9, Paul exhorted Timothy, "Exhort bondservants to be obedient to their own masters, to be well pleasing in all things, not answering back." Then he continues in verse 10, "not pilfering." While being a bond-servant in the first century is not exactly the same as being an employee in the twenty-first century, the principle is the same: don't steal. Pilfering or stealing could involve something as minor as paper clips or as major as cash. It would also involve time. Time improperly handled could bring a fellow employee to Christ but drive a non-Christian employer further from Him because of a Christian's misuse of work time. Being used of God in the work-place involves the use of your time in the most God-honoring way.

So serving Christ in the workplace doesn't mean slacking off on the job. How do we balance our obligations to our employer and our commitment to share Christ? The Bible tells us how to get to heaven. It also tells us how to take those in the workplace along with us. So when considering how to impact the workplace for Christ, the Bible is the place to start.

Sandwiched in five verses in Colossians 4:2–6 is sufficient guidance for anyone who wants to make an eternal impact on those he or she rubs shoulders with every day. In this letter written by the apostle Paul to first-century believers in the Greek city of Colosse are a number of admonitions regarding work. In Colossians 3:22–4:1 Paul directly addressed a class of believers who were the most common workers of the day, bondservants or slaves:

> Bondservants, obey in all things your masters according to the flesh, not with eyeservice, as men-pleasers, but in sincerity of heart, fearing God. And whatever you do, do it heartily, as to the Lord and not to men, knowing that from the Lord you will receive the reward of the inheritance; for you serve the Lord Christ. But he who does wrong will be repaid for what he has done, and there is no partiality. Masters, give your bondservants what is just and fair, knowing that you also have a Master in heaven.

Just because they were Christians wasn't an excuse for laziness or carelessness. It's not about trying to please the master when he's looking. It's about pleasing God who sees everything all the time. Whatever the position or task in which they were employed, Paul encourages them to do their work as if they were working for the Lord Himself.

Christian masters were admonished as well: don't misuse or abuse your servants. Do what is just and treat them fairly. You may be in charge now, but ultimately God has the final say as your boss. The master will answer to God on the basis of his treatment of his slaves.

As we've noted, the first-century world of slaves and servants wasn't the same as the modern-day workplace. Slaves couldn't change jobs, seek better working conditions, or rely on laws to protect their status in the workplace. Paul does, however, touch upon principles of work that apply even today. Our motivation for work should go beyond just doing the job. As Christians, what we do at work can bring about eternal benefit. Likewise for employers and supervisors—how we treat others is noticed by God. Justice and fairness are not optional.

Having set the stage for a discussion of work roles, Paul follows this section of his letter with three directives in Colossians 4:2–6 that apply to many areas but most importantly to the workplace. In the chapters that follow we'll examine each of these three imperatives in more detail. In our study of this passage we want to answer two basic questions: (1) What does this mean? and (2) How does it apply to the workplace?

Based on those answers, we want to further look at what we need to know to evangelize effectively in the workplace. Many Christians have a lot of credibility because they've lived the Christian life before others as they should. They may not, however, have examined carefully enough the message they are sharing with lost people. We ought not speak with confusion where God speaks with clarity. We'll explore how to turn conversations to spiritual things and present the gospel with clarity and simplicity. We'll also examine how to help new believers "grow in the grace and knowledge of our Lord and Savior Jesus Christ" (2 Peter 3:18). Then, having discussed those areas, we'll examine how what we have learned can be transferred into public speaking opportunities. Believers in a variety of workplaces may fail to see the public speaking opportunities available to them.

I have a friend who is active in the Marines. The good thing is, he's never found out he's in the Marines! By that I mean he sees himself as someone in full-time service for the Lord, stationed in the Marine Corp. He is outspoken about his trust in Christ, incorporates it into public speaking opportunities, and has regularly seen people come to know Jesus Christ. The full impact of how God has used him will only be seen when he is one day with the Lord. There is no question in my mind he'll be abundantly rewarded for how God has used him in full-time ministry in the military. Not every believer may have the same opportunities, but all believers have some opportunities.

Conclusion

Your workplace is not merely your job; it's your ministry. Let's discuss how we can use that job to populate heaven. In so doing, you will have had the greatest ministry you could possibly have. Your workplace will not only be the means of meeting temporal needs like putting food on the table or providing funds for a vacation. It will also count for something eternal—introducing those you work with to the only One who can give them life that never ends.

Part I

Pray as You Should

*Continue earnestly in prayer, being vigilant
in it with thanksgiving.*
—Colossians 4:2

Chapter One

What Does That Mean?

Prayer is not where you end your ministry in the workplace. It's where your ministry begins. If anything of a spiritual nature is going to happen, God has to do it. Ministry in the workplace is God-sized. Christ's words in John 15:5 dare not be forgotten: "Without Me you can do nothing." Two things are essential.

Pray, and keep on praying.

Notice how Paul began his exhortation in Colossians 4:2: "Continue earnestly in prayer, being vigilant in it with thanksgiving." The idea behind words like "continue earnestly" and "being vigilant" is that prayer ought to come from our lips like water comes from a dripping faucet. Pray when you get up and pray an hour after you're up. Pray before breakfast and pray after breakfast. Pray on your way to work and pray on your way home. Pray before your sales appointment and pray afterward. Pray as you leave the warehouse and pray as you return. Pray as you open up your e-mails and pray as you press "send." Bottom line: make it a habit to engage in consistent prayer.

Paul's emphasis on prayer is like the boy who always wanted a baby brother. His dad told him, "The only way you can get anything is to ask God for it—so if you want a baby brother, you'll have to ask God for one." So morning, noon, and night the boy prayed. He prayed before breakfast and after breakfast; on his way to school and on his way home; before soccer practice and after soccer practice. There was never an hour he didn't pray. After several weeks of praying, he still did not have a baby brother. So he thought, *This isn't doing any good*, and he stopped praying. Nine months later his father said, "Son, your mother is going to the hospital and I think when she comes home, she'll have God's answer to your prayers in her arms." Sure enough, when the mother came home, she not only had one new little brother in her arms, but two, beautiful twin boys. The father, wanting to drive his lesson home, said, "Son, aren't you glad you prayed the way you did?" To which the son answered, "I sure am, Dad, but aren't you glad I stopped when I did?"

Like that little boy, we should pray daily and hourly. But unlike him, our commitment to prayer shouldn't end after a few weeks of effort. Every day and every situation of that day presents us with opportunities to stay in communication with our Lord.

How does one pray as he sends an invoice, drives to his next sales job, or greets his next client? The answer is to live in an atmosphere of prayer. God hears the whispers of the heart, and a person can pray just as earnestly while changing the sparkplugs of a car as one does when participating in a prayer group at church. This doesn't mean that having a time and place each day when we regularly meet with the Lord isn't important. The point is, God is never more than a prayer breath away. We can bring everything to Him in prayer as it comes to us in life.

———

I've often been asked how a busy person keeps from being distracted as he prays. It's hard to pause and pray when you're facing a deadline on a project, or there's an appointment you have yet to prepare for. You may feel overwhelmed by concerns on the home front that you carry with you to work, or your work schedule seems to master you instead of you mastering it. What do we do to work effectively without losing focus?

The answer is twofold. First, speak to God about the distractions. God has no limits on what we can bring before Him. That means we can come to Him and say, "Help me when I talk to you not to get distracted." This is another one of those areas in our lives where He can do "exceedingly abundantly above all that we ask or think" (Eph. 3:20). Second, putting Him where He needs to be has a way of putting everything else where it needs to be. A businessman friend of mine said to me, "I've found something very interesting. When I take the time I need to spend with the Lord, everything I was concerned about getting done somehow gets done."

That's right—it's a God thing! Putting Him in His rightful place in our priorities has a way of helping us get everything else in order. We can get done whatever needs to be done as He shows what is necessary and what can wait until another day. Perhaps that is what made Martin Luther say, "I have so much to do today that I shall spend the first three hours in prayer."[1]

Accompany prayer with thanks.

Prayer is not merely talking to God about doing something, but also thanking Him for what He's already done. It should not surprise anyone that Paul also said, "with thanksgiving."

"Thanksgiving" is not a P.S. attached to the end of a prayer. It's a spirit in which our requests are made. We pray to a God of grace, One from whose hand we deserve nothing but the just punishment for our sins. Instead, He holds back from us what we rightly deserve so He might give us what we don't deserve.

We're thankful for who He is. The psalmist said, "Praise the LORD! Oh, give thanks to the LORD, for He is good! For His mercy endures forever" (Ps. 106:1). We're thankful for who we are in Him. Paul exhorted the Colossians, "Giving thanks to the Father who has qualified us to be partakers of the inheritance of the saints in the light. He has delivered us from the power of darkness and conveyed us into the kingdom of the Son of His love, in whom we have redemption through His blood, the forgiveness of sins" (Col. 1:12–14).

We're thankful for everything good that comes from His

hand—the physical as well as the spiritual. Paul made that clear by rebuking those who set up rigid rules about the physical as if spiritual things were all that mattered. He wrote to his young protégé Timothy:

> Now the Spirit expressly says that in latter times some will depart from the faith, giving heed to deceiving spirits and doctrines of demons, speaking lies in hypocrisy, having their own conscience seared with a hot iron, forbidding to marry, and commanding to abstain from foods which God created to be received with thanksgiving by those who believe and know the truth. For every creature of God is good, and nothing is to be refused if it is received with thanksgiving; for it is sanctified by the word of God and prayer. (1 Tim. 4:1–5)

Prayer is all-inclusive. As Paul told the Thessalonians, "In everything give thanks; for this is the will of God in Christ Jesus for you" (1 Thess. 5:18).

KEY POINTS

Two essentials that dare not be neglected are:

- Pray, and keep on praying.
- Accompany prayer with thanks.

These two alone can make a phenomenal difference as you begin ministry each day in the workplace. You'll soon realize that what has happened through your nine-to-five day can only be attributed to the supernatural.

Chapter Two

What Do We Pray For?

Prayer is not mouthing words; it's speaking to God. It's talking to Him in such a way that a load that was pressing on your shoulders has now been transferred to His. What do you transfer to His shoulders? What do you ask God for?

Whatever our job or career, we can be engaged in evangelism in the workplace. That does not mean, however, that the responsibility for results depends entirely upon us. It doesn't. There are five things God provides. They aren't natural provisions—they are supernatural ones.

Opportunity

As I will keep emphasizing throughout this book—your job is your ministry, your ministry is your job. Any worker yielded to God can walk through an open door, but the open door is a God thing. Lewis Sperry Chafer said it well: "The divine order is to talk to God about men, until the door is definitely open to talk to men about God."[1] No one recognized that any better than the apostle Paul. What he said about an open door for his ministry applies just as well for open doors for your ministry. As I will keep emphasizing throughout this book—your job is your ministry, your ministry is your job.

Does the Bible encourage us to pray for such opportunities? Definitely! Colossians 4:3 is a clear affirmation of this. As Paul was under house arrest, he undoubtedly had opportunities to share the gospel. Had I been a non-Christian Roman guard, it could have been exhausting to be chained (which often was the practice) to Paul for twenty-four hours a day! His desire was that he not be limited by his confinement. So, on behalf of himself and all of his associates, he requested prayer that "God would open to us a door for the word." Acts 28:30–31 relates how God answered those prayers. If Paul couldn't go out to reach the citizens of Rome, then God would send Romans to Paul! For two years, a continual stream of visitors came to Paul's rented quarters and heard the gospel. And so did the Roman guards who constantly stood on duty!

Lydia is another exciting example of what God can do to open doors in the workplace. She was a businesswoman in the Greek city of Philippi and the first Christian convert in Europe. Luke relates the story of her conversion in Acts 16:11–15:

> Therefore, sailing from Troas, we ran a straight course to Samothrace, and the next day came to Neapolis, and from there to Philippi, which is the foremost city of that part of Macedonia, a colony. And we were staying in that city for some days. And on the Sabbath day we went out of the city to the riverside, where prayer was customarily made; and we sat down and spoke to the women who met there. Now a certain woman named Lydia heard us. She was a seller of purple from the city of Thyatira, who worshiped God. The Lord opened her heart to heed the things spoken by Paul. And when she and her household were baptized, she begged us, saying, "If you have judged me to be faithful to the Lord, come to my house and stay." So she persuaded us.

Lydia came from a region in Asia Minor called by the same name. Apparently, she was so closely tied to that region that her personal name was the name of her native province. Five large cities comprise that part of Asia Minor—Ephesus, Smyrna, Sardis, Philadelphia, and Thyatira. All five cities were near chief rivers and had good roads connecting them. The "Lydian Market" was known for generations throughout the Graeco-Roman world for its wide and valuable trade.

Lydia, a native of Thyatira of western Asia Minor, conducted her business at Philippi, a city of eastern Macedonia on the east-west Egnatia Highway between Rome and Asia. She walked the streets of Philippi as a "seller of purple [goods]." This "purple" was either purple-dyed textiles or a secretion of a species of murex or mollusk from which a purple dye was made. The juice of the shellfish was white while still in its veins, but once it was exposed to the sun, it could range from a purplish blue to a crimson color. No doubt she wore purple herself, which would have been in keeping with a merchant selling this expensive product. Her customers probably included Babylonian buyers who bought their purple to use in making temple curtains or making costumes for their idols. Some costumes were probably purchased for the Roman Imperial family, who wore the imperial purple on state occasions.

Lydia was part of a group of worshipers that met on the bank of the Gangites River. Ten Jewish men were required to form a synagogue, so the fact that these women were meeting by the river meant that there were very few Jewish men in the city. Getting away from the city offered them the solitude (and perhaps safety) needed to worship. Lydia, the successful businesswoman, was a Gentile, but she worshiped the one God of the Jews and longing to know God better, she was at the place of prayer and worship on the Sabbath.

Religious people are sometimes the hardest to reach. Note what the text tells us: "The Lord opened her heart to heed the things spoken by Paul." Paul proclaimed the good news of Christ's death and resurrection—the gospel that was now speeding west into Macedonia. Paul proclaimed the gospel and Lydia, whose heart had been opened by God, responded in faith. As a testimony to her faith, she and her household were baptized. Her hunger for truth was such that she invited Paul and Silas to come to her house. Although reluctant to impose upon her, Paul explains, "She persuaded us." One can only imagine how many hours Paul spent teaching these new converts in the warmth of her home.

Lydia appears unashamed of her newfound faith, so much so that she opened her doors to Paul when he was supernaturally delivered from prison (Acts 16:40). No doubt she was foremost on his mind when he wrote his letter to the Philippians and addressed the group Lydia had helped assemble. He said, "I thank my God upon every remembrance of you, always in every prayer of mine making request for you all with joy, for your fellowship in the gospel from the first day until now" (Phil. 1:3–5).

What's the point of all of these details? First, so that you can see that Lydia was someone prominent in the workplace of her day. Second, so that you see clearly that she responded to the gospel because the Lord opened her heart. Paul and Silas walked through the door that God opened.

God is more concerned about the lost people we work with than we are. Therefore, we should pray with expectation for a door of opportunity. As we do so, we should recognize that a door of opportunity may come much faster than we ever anticipated.

While speaking in Missouri, a businessman excitedly told me that while on a recent business trip, he sat next to an elderly woman on the plane. As soon as he sat down, the woman asked him if he believed in Satan. That immediately began a discussion of spiritual things. He found the woman to be most receptive and attentive. After he explained the gospel to her, she said that she needed some time to think about what he had shared. Apparently, she brought up Satan because of something that had just happened to her. Doors of opportunity may come sooner than we think and in unexpected ways.

Boldness

The workplace is a great place to engage in conversation. Whether during coffee breaks, the lunch hour, or during some "down time" with a co-worker, a conversation can easily turn from events of the night before to plans for the evening ahead. Subjects include children, marital conflicts, birthdays, vacations, home projects, lawn mowing, accidents, relatives, rumors, landscaping, exercising, and sports. The list is seemingly endless. Many of these topics offer opportunities to transition into spiritual things. All of a sudden there is that fear sensation—sweating palms, shaking knees and hearts, nervous tongue. You recognize that the present moment may not be appropriate to delve into spiritual things. As I stated earlier, an employer is paying you to work, not witness. But you could at least open the door to further conversation. How do you overcome that fear—fear that anyone who's honest would tell you they face when witnessing in the workplace?

In Ephesians 6:19–20 Paul provides us with a great example of how to overcome fear. He requested prayer for two items—both so tightly connected that they're inseparable. The first he called "utterance." As he writes to the Ephesian believers, he requested prayer that "utterance may be given to me." The word *utterance* simply means that when I open my mouth, something will come out of it. Who cannot identify with such a request? Paul asked for prayer that he would have the ability to speak up and not clam up!

Mercedes Benz is known to build vehicles so well engineered that they have saved the lives of many people. Even though Mercedes holds the patent on many safety features, competitors are free to use them because the company does not enforce its claim on the patent. When asked why, one Mercedes spokesman is reported to have said, "Because some things in life are too important not to share."[2] The message of the gospel is too important not to share. The comfort we have is that God knows that more than we do. Therefore, we can ask God to open our mouths in such a way that the message that needs to come out can't stay in. We can pray and enlist others to pray for us that we'll be able to speak when there is an opportunity.

Paul does not stop there. Not only did he request prayer that something would come out of his mouth, he requested prayer that what came out would come out boldly. The use of "that" designates a second request in addition to utterance. He continued, ". . . that I may open my mouth boldly to make known the mystery of the gospel." The "mystery of the gospel" Paul was referring to was not some deep, dark secret known only to a select few. It was the new reality that Jews and Gentiles were one in the body of Christ. Paul did not merely want to open his mouth and state a fact—he wanted to proclaim it boldly. He even repeated that need when he continued, ". . . that in it I may speak boldly, as I ought to speak."

The issue is never the fear to speak on behalf of the Savior. Fear is normal. Rejection is possible. Those who constantly speak on behalf of Christ in the workplace are not without fear. They are the ones who go ahead in spite of fear. Boldness overcomes fear instead of fear overcoming boldness. Why? Instead of merely talking to others about their fear, they speak to God. They also ask others, as Paul did, to speak to God on their behalf, asking Him to give them needed boldness. A God who has promised to answer prayers that are in accordance with His will (1 John 5:14–15) will provide greater boldness than we ever dreamed we would have.

My wife, Tammy, is a prime example. She is known as a person who is always fearful but always talking on behalf of the Savior. Her activity in evangelism is a walking answer to prayer. She asks God for boldness and requests that others pray for her as well. Boldness has conquered fear instead of fear conquering boldness.

Fellow believers pray for you and for issues related to your job, don't they? They may pray for a better relationship with your supervisor, a needed raise, better working conditions, or safety as you work. How often have you said to them, "Pray that as I have an opportunity to speak on behalf of Christ, something may come out of my mouth and that what comes out may come out boldly"?

Success

Another item believers in the workplace need to pray for will actually reach beyond the workplace. And that is . . . success! Understanding how such a prayer request is presented in Scripture will help us understand how success in witnessing in the workplace reaches beyond the workplace.

In chapter three of Paul's second letter to the Thessalonian believers, he explained what his request was for himself. He began in verse one, "Finally, brethren, pray for us, that the word of the

Lord may run swiftly and be glorified, just as it is with you." The phrase "word of the Lord" is a figure of speech referring to the message of the gospel. "Run swiftly" is a colorful and very active figure of speech. Words don't literally "run," but Paul wanted the gospel to speed forward like a sprinter! This phrase is often translated "spread rapidly."

We can see just how rapidly the gospel spread throughout Thessalonica by reading Acts 17:1–4 where we're told:

> Now when they had passed through Amphipolis and Apollonia, they came to Thessalonica, where there was a synagogue of the Jews. Then Paul, as his custom was, went in to them, and for three Sabbaths reasoned with them from the Scriptures, explaining and demonstrating that the Christ had to suffer and rise again from the dead, and saying, "This Jesus whom I preach to you is the Christ." And some of them were persuaded; and a great multitude of the devout Greeks, and not a few of the leading women, joined Paul and Silas.

Paul's ministry in Thessalonica resulted in major impact! Verse four specifically says, "A great multitude of the devout Greeks, and not a few of the leading women." Paul's statement in 2 Thessalonians 3:1—"just as it is with you"—needed no further explanation to the Thessalonians. They knew firsthand what he was talking about.

When we read about these believers in Paul's first letter, we get a clear picture of how the gospel spread. First Thessalonians 1:6–9 tells us that they not only received Paul's message, they joyfully became faithful followers, in spite of being persecuted for their faith. They in turn became examples to other believers. Paul says that people everywhere were talking about how the gospel had changed their lives. They had turned from the worship of idols to the worship of the living God, and that news had spread like wildfire. The gospel went beyond just the people Paul knew. It went to the people the Thessalonians knew that Paul didn't.

Carry that thought into the workplace. You share the gospel with a co-worker who trusts Christ. That person, now a new believer, burdened for his or her relatives and friends, tells them the same good news you shared. The gospel has a ripple effect. As God opens lost people's hearts, a multitude could come to Christ.

This is the kind of success we ought to pray for in the workplace. God wants the gospel to spread throughout the factory, the office, the hair salon, and the mechanic shop. He wants it to go beyond those walls to the community in which employees live, to the families they represent, and to the relationships they have with neighbors and friends. Our prayer should be for the gospel to run!

Safety

Witnessing can be rewarding, but it can also be dangerous. After all, you're making a direct attack against Satan's kingdom. Speaking to a co-worker about the weather or an upcoming trip is safe territory. Satan is delighted when such mundane conversations are the norm. But speak to a person about his or her need for Christ, and Satan goes all out to oppose the message and the messenger. This is the reason that the Bible says, "Yes, and all who desire to live godly in Christ Jesus will suffer persecution" (2 Tim. 3:12). Anyone who lives a godly life in obedience to Christ is not a silent witness. Persecution of one kind or another is to be expected.

Paul understood this reality only too well. After he requested prayer for success in 2 Thessalonians 3, he requested prayer for safety—"that we may be delivered from unreasonable and wicked men; for not all have faith" (v. 2). The Greek word translated here as "unreasonable" goes beyond the way they think to include the idea of perverseness—men capable of harmful acts—while "wickedness" points to their conduct. Evil people do evil things. The reason is, "For not all have faith." A change on the inside has to precede a change on the outside.

Acts 18:12–13 tells us of the persecution Paul encountered in Corinth: "When Gallio was proconsul of Achaia, the Jews with one accord rose up against Paul and brought him to the judgment seat, saying, 'This fellow persuades men to worship God contrary to the law.'" Since Gallio was relatively new in this important political position, the Jewish leaders saw their opportunity. If they could persuade him to make Christianity illegal, all Christians could be persecuted legally. Paul knew the reality of what the apostle John wrote: "He who is in you is greater than he who is in the world" (1 John 4:4). Paul's refuge was not revenge—it was prayer.

There may not be persecution in the workplace itself, but persecution may come from places that impact the workplace—a union may establish intimidating work rules; the threat of a supervisor or manager that "there could be consequences;" or even a legal ruling by a court that infringes upon a person's right of free speech. Safety may not be a need now, but it could be needed at any time in the future. The time to pray for safety is sooner, not later. Satan often works behind the scenes now to cause harm or mayhem in the future.

Salvation

In the New Testament the emphasis of prayer in evangelism is for the believers who are sharing the gospel. As we've discovered, we ought to pray for opportunity, boldness, safety, and success. But prayer ought not stop there. We are to pray for the object of our evangelism—the unbelievers.

The clearest passage in the New Testament that encourages us to pray for lost people is 1 Timothy 2. Paul says in his letter to his young protégé, Timothy: "Therefore I exhort first of all that supplications, prayers, intercessions, and giving of thanks be made for all men" (v. 1). Note that Paul does not say "all Christians." He says "all men" (by which he means all people). Paul continues, "For this is good and acceptable in the sight of God our Savior, who desires all men to be saved and to come to the knowledge of the truth" (vv. 3–4). The point in 1 Timothy 2:1–4 is unmistakable: we are to pray for lost people. What is foremost in God's mind ought to be foremost in ours—the salvation of the lost.

Believers are to talk to the lost about Christ, and we are to talk to Christ about the lost. We are to ask God to show the lost their need of Him, give them an understanding of His death and resurrection, and bring them to Himself. And we need to pray expectantly. We can do so because we know that God loves them more than we do. Regardless of how deeply we want them to come to Christ, His yearnings for them are even stronger than ours.

A pastor wrote to me and shared the following testimony: "One of our single ladies called from work to tell us about a young lady that worked with her who came into work upset and was asking all kinds of questions about the Bible and Jesus. A close friend had died, and she was really upset. Our church member, besides praying for her, had shared Christ with the woman in the past, and now that the chips were down, the co-worker came seeking help. It was about 6:00 p.m. when our church member called. She was nervous that she would make a mistake, and she was also tied up in a project that her boss had told her she needed to finish. She called to see if I could come to work and meet the woman in the break room. Well, I wasn't home, so my wife called our visitation pastor and he was also gone. She then called the youth pastor, and he was home. He said that he would go meet with the woman. He met with her and one hour later, she trusted Christ." Pray for the salvation of the lost.

KEY POINTS

When it comes to what to pray for in the workplace regarding evangelism, the Bible gives specifics. Pray for:

- Opportunity—God has to open the door
- Boldness—ask God for the courage that overcomes fear
- Safety—ask God for protection
- Success—pray that the gospel will spread rapidly
- Salvation—ask God to bring the lost to Himself

We honor God in evangelism not just by talking to people about God but also by talking to God about people. The privilege is overwhelming, and since God is a prayer-answering God, the results are as well.

Chapter Three

What Do Open Doors Look Like?

Spiritual open doors have one thing in common with physical open doors (the kind that hang on a hinge). They don't all come in the same color and they don't all look alike. But when you "knock" on them, you often find that they are doors that will open to you.

Where are doors of opportunity often found in the workplace?

Prayer Groups

A CEO I once visited provides a room at the office for those who want to meet for prayer before beginning work. Believers in the company who accept his offer often lead other employees to Christ who meet with them for prayer. They discover in conversations with these co-workers that they do not actually know the Lord. Although they were God-fearing in that they wanted to honor Him in prayer, they had missed the simple gospel message.

Bible Studies

A bank executive received permission from his boss to hold a weekly Bible study prior to work hours. Several began attending, and he had a chance to talk boldly about spiritual things. I have known of numerous Bible studies that result in people coming to know Christ. I personally led such a study in a hotel. The owner, a personal friend of mine, requested I do so. We met once a week on Thursday mornings from 7 a.m. to 8 a.m. There are men today in Dallas who were saved because they were brought to that study by concerned Christian businesspeople.

Meal Times

Non-Christians have at least one thing in common with believers. They eat! Sometimes too much—like all of us! But that one-to-one time across the lunch table allows them to open up about spiritual things in a way they often wouldn't do in their homes before their spouses and families. Often I've been privileged to be in on their conversions. A worker concerned about a co-worker asked me to go to lunch with the two of them because of the co-worker's interest in spiritual things. There at the lunch table, the non-Christian passed from darkness into light. The new believer left the lunch table knowing he had tasted the Bread of Life, something far more superior and eternal than the physical bread he had received. The same can be said about dinner invitations, whether at home or at a restaurant. The spouse of the co-worker could also be invited. By enjoying the comforts of your home, you might have the opportunity to invite them to the comfort of His home.

Carpooling

Sometimes the privilege of talking about spiritual things doesn't happen within the confines of the office building, but within the confines of a car that transports co-workers to the office building. Carpooling often provides the chance to talk to someone for whom you've been praying that you might have a door of opportunity. The transition might come as you drive past the beauty of an outdoor park, reflect upon a statement on a billboard, talk about the previous Sunday church service, or simply allude to something you've been praying about. The privacy of an automobile is often used of the Lord to transport people not merely to work but into a relationship with Christ.

Special Events

A local church may sponsor a special event that Christians in the workplace can invite non-Christians to attend. For example, I came to Christ through my interest of the outdoors and specifically through the sport of hunting. Seeing the wonders of nature and the way God made it all made me say, "He's there—but where?" I decided to study the Bible and came to Christ through my own Bible study as God took me from the creation, to the Creator, and then to Christ.

I often speak at Wild Game Feasts sponsored by a church for the community. After a 45-minute PowerPoint presentation of my hunting experiences, I give my testimony—"Hunting wildlife and finding God." Many Christians bring their workplace acquaintances who enjoy the outdoors. We range from a minimum of 40 percent to 60 or even 80 percent non-Christians in attendance. Events like these are God-given, wide-open doors for the gospel. Other possibilities include father-son retreats, mother-daughter banquets, and marriage retreats. The list of possibilities is extensive.

Loaning Books

People don't read as much as they used to, but many do read. So the sharing of books is another opportunity. Note that I use the word *sharing*, not *giving*. When you share a book, you can solicit a response. It's appropriate to say, "I want to share a book with you because it's meant a lot to me spiritually. I'd like to know what you think but I'll need it back in a month. Would you like to read it?" It ought to be one that causes non-Christians to think about who Christ is and what the cross and resurrection are all about. It should be thought provoking, easy to follow, biblically sound, and on their wavelength—that's the kind of book you offer to share with nonbelievers.

Christian Literature

Beyond books there is a great variety of Christian literature you can make available to others. Those who are CEOs or executives of a company often have the best opportunities to reach a number of people. Sometimes they have the sole authority to decide what to make available for non-Christians to read. For example, hotel managers have placed our booklet, "May I Ask You a Question?" on their registration desk; doctors have placed it on the tables of their waiting rooms; insurance executives on the tables in their lobby; and owners of car dealerships at the customer service desk. I even spoke to the CEO of a cancer laboratory that makes evangelistic literature available in his reception area.

Every Christian in the workplace clearly should carry an attractive tract that presents the gospel. If you ask God for opportunities, you may not know where or how they may come, but be ready. They will come! Sometimes they just seem to "pop up" in the most unexpected places. It may not even be in your workplace. It may be people you come across when you are at their workplace. After all, as a disciple of Christ in the workplace, your whole lifestyle should be that of wanting to influence lost people wherever you go.

Several years ago prior to Christmas, my wife, Tammy, was in a grocery store. While at the deli counter waiting for service, she asked the woman standing next to her if she was ready for Christmas. They started chatting, and Tammy said, "I have a booklet I'd love to share with you," and handed her one of our "May I Ask You a Question?" tracts. The woman began to read, and asked, "Where do you go to church?" The woman then explained that some cultists had come by and asked her to visit their church. Tammy responded, "Well, I'd love to get together and explain the booklet to you if you're interested." The woman expressed an interest and gave Tammy her phone number. Days later, Tammy visited with her in her apartment and had the privilege of leading her to Christ.

As you pray for opportunities, watch out—they will be there!

Personal Testimony

An unbeliever might be able to argue about what you believe, but it's difficult to argue about what's happened to you that's biblically based. Your testimony can be shared during informal conversations that can play a part in opening doors for the gospel, whether it's during the car pool, in the break room at a lunch table, or at appropriate company functions. A non-Christian may hear you and think, "Jesus Christ has changed his life. I wonder if He could change mine?"

As with all presentations of the gospel, it's essential that you be clear. Your testimony needs to clearly explain how you came to understand that: (1) you're a sinner, (2) Christ died for you and rose again, and (3) only through personal faith in Him can we receive the free gift of eternal life.

Personal Notes and Favors

In a day when relationships can be stymied by coldness and indifference, people respond to heart-felt notes such as:

Sorry about the passing of your sister—my prayers are with you.
Get well soon—we miss you at work.
I know the last four months have been difficult on your home front—I hope things are getting better as I pray for you.
Sorry to hear about your accident but so glad you were not injured.

Notes like these go a long way in saying "I care."

Along with these personal expressions, look for opportunities to extend personal favors: a ride to work while their car is in the shop; helping clean up the yard after the onslaught of a storm; or mowing the yard while they take a much needed vacation. The more "out of the way" it takes you, the more it shouts, "I'm here and I care."

Sincere Comments

One other possibility is so obvious and yet so overlooked. Doors of opportunity don't always come in large time slots or during extended conversations. Sometimes they come in the simplest remarks that open up doors later. A doctor friend of mine loves to say to his patients, "I have a feeling someone upstairs has been watching over you." It is thrilling to hear later how that simple remark has opened up doors for the gospel.

An executive I know, as he prepares to eat lunch, often says to his waitress, "We're about to thank God for the food. Is there something we could pray with you about?" He has never had a negative response. That remark has allowed him to leave a generous tip and booklet that explains the gospel. While traveling, I've conversed with people who have shared something heavy on their minds or hearts. After expressing concern, I've said, "I'll say a word of prayer for you." The most common response I receive is, "Thanks" or "I appreciate that" or "I could sure use that." That has allowed me to respond then or at a later time and talk about the One to whom I'm praying.

KEY POINTS

Doors of opportunity: Many—Varied—Expected—Unexpected.

They are:

- Prayer groups
- Bible studies
- Meal times
- Carpooling
- Special events
- Loaning books
- Christian literature
- Personal testimony

- Personal notes and favors
- Sincere comments

As you become increasingly alert to opportunities, you may become increasingly frustrated. But it will be one of the most exciting frustrations you have ever had. Instead of asking, "Where do I find the time and opportunity?" you will find yourself asking, "Which opportunity do I take advantage of first?"

Part 2

Live as You Should

Walk in wisdom toward those who are outside,
redeeming the time.
—Colossians 4:5

Chapter Four

What Does That Mean?

The comment arrested my attention. I was studying for my Doctor of Ministry degree from Gordon Conwell seminary in Boston, Massachusetts. A lecturer one day mentioned the results of a survey taken among believers in the workplace. They were asked a rather simple question: "Why don't you witness to others you work alongside of as you have the opportunity?" One answer was more prominent than all the others. It was: "Because I haven't lived the life I should."

It impacts the person's openness and boldness to witness. When they approach a situation where there may be an opportunity to witness, they are most likely thinking, "I can't bring up spiritual issues. What if they find out how I live compared to how I talk?"

The biblical remedy is rather simple and direct—live the way you should. Live in obedience to God and in keeping with the way He has called believers to live. In Colossians 4:5 Paul wrote, "Walk in wisdom toward those who are outside, redeeming the time." What exactly does that mean?

"Walk"

Walk in this context does not refer, of course, to physically moving our feet as in walking to the breakfast table. Rather, it refers to the way we live from breakfast table to breakfast table— our way of living. The word *walk* is a metaphor for our lifestyle. It includes anything and everything people may observe about us—our interactions with our neighbors, the integrity we exhibit by the promises we make and keep, and the way we treat the people we dislike or who dislike us. It includes the patience or irritability we exhibit as we stand in line at the grocery store or airport security or the way we put others before ourselves.

In the workplace it may be the way we speak about the boss behind his back, the way we treat a fellow employee, or the generosity we extend to a fellow worker who we know is hurting financially. It includes our quickness to forgive someone in our department for his demeaning remarks and our integrity or lack of it with which we perform our job or conduct business. It's not where we walk that Paul had in mind—it's how we walk. The Bible's exhortation to "Be holy, for I am holy" (1 Peter 1:16) is something to take seriously, not lightly. Jesus said in Matthew 5:16 that we are to let our light shine before others. A life compromised by disobedience to God makes a very dim light.

"Wisdom"

Wisdom means discernment gained through the development of godly character. It is akin to the wisdom mentioned in Proverbs. It is a skill for living your life the way God wants you to live it and that ability is gained by experience and maturity in our walk with God. So Paul is saying, "Live your life daily with spiritual discernment, making choices that go along with what He is teaching you as you walk with Him." An old Persian proverb says, "For every pound of learning a person does, he needs ten pounds of common sense to know how to use it." You might define this wisdom as taking the spiritually imparted common sense God is giving you as you walk with Him and properly using it to impact the lost.

Wisdom is spiritual discernment demonstrated day by day, incident by incident, step by step as we walk with Him. It means we do the good and godly thing. When we don't, we apologize and ask for forgiveness; learn from our mistakes; and continue forward.

"Redeeming the Time"

Redeeming the time means grasping the opportunity. Napoleon once stated that the reason he defeated the Austrians is that they never learned the value of five minutes. Paul is saying, "Learn the value of five minutes." Don't miss the opportunity to let your life support your lips. Your life should always be a help to your message, not a hindrance. Live in such a way that you draw non-Christians closer to Jesus instead of turning them away from Him.

So we could paraphrase Colossians 4:5 by saying, "Walk with godly discernment in relation to those who don't know the Lord, taking advantage of every opportunity to influence them for Christ." Live as you should, and as others look at your life, they will be prompted to say:

"Whatever she has, I want."
"I feel safe talking to him about a work issue."
"I think I can trust her to be fair."
"He seems interested in all of us."
"What makes her different?"
"I wish I could be like him."
"I think she must be a Christian—at least she lives like one."

Paul stated the same truth in another way when he wrote to Titus in the same passage we looked at earlier. He says, "Exhort bondservants to be obedient to their own masters, to be well pleasing in all things, not answering back, not pilfering, but showing all good fidelity, that they may adorn the doctrine of God our Savior in all things" (Titus 2:9–10).

As we noted earlier, Paul is speaking directly to a culture where slavery was the norm, not the exception. While the context is not the same, the principles apply to the employee/employer relationship today. Christian workers should be committed to following Christ in the workplace so that their lives prove to be an adornment of the teachings of Christ. As a Christmas ornament decorates a tree and calls attention to it, our lives should call attention to the teachings of Christ and cause others to be properly impressed. Friedrich Nietzsche, the atheistic German philosopher who became famous in the late 1800s for proclaiming that God was dead, once said, "They would have to sing better songs for me to learn to have faith in their Redeemer; and his disciples would have to look more redeemed!" Like a supporting beam in a house, our lives become a support of the message that goes out from our lips.

One word of caution, however. There are those who may say, "We don't have to say anything—just living the Christian life is our witness." Nothing could be further from the truth. The most perfectly lived life does not tell a person how to come to Christ. Living the life should not become an excuse for not evangelizing. Sooner or later, someone needs to speak to a lost person. The way we live is a support to the message we share, not a substitute for the message.

KEY POINTS

Henry Stanley said of the missionary explorer David Livingston, "He never tried to convert me but had I lived with him any longer I would have become a Christian."[1] We should so live that others would be forced to say, "If I spend much more time with you, I'm likely to become a Christian." That means:

- Walk with godly discernment in relation to non-Christians
- Grasp every opportunity to influence them for Christ

Let your life draw them closer to Christ, not drive them from Him.

Chapter Five

What Does This Look Like in the Workplace?

Knowing what we need to do is one thing. Doing it is another. If belief doesn't come through in one's behavior, someone could rightly ask, "How strongly do you believe that?" When belief does come through in behavior, it causes a non-Christian to ask, "I wonder what it is about him that makes him behave the way he does. I'm impressed."

Randy Kilgore, in his book *Talking About God in the Twenty-First Century Marketplace,* comments, "When an employer, co-worker, or customer trusts your daily work efforts, he is more likely to trust your spiritual efforts also."[1] So to determine if we're living the kind of life that we should be living, what kind of questions should we ask ourselves?

Am I a good worker?

As I interact with CEOs and managers across the country, one struggle continually comes up—"It's hard to find good workers. They want the benefits but not the work." Good, competent workers are increasingly hard to find. An employer, however, needs to ask, "Am I the type of person I'm asking my employee to be?

employees?"

From an employee standpoint, the same struggle may apply. Workers can be just as frustrated with an employer's lack of a good work ethic. As employees, however, each of us needs to examine our own job performance. "Am I working as hard as I would like my supervisor to work?" Encouragement validated by example is always the most powerful motivator of change in others.

Do I act and react with self-control?

It's not just about how we act, but also about how we react. We've all heard it said, "You cannot help what happens to you, but you can help what you do about it." Another way of putting it is, "You cannot always control what happens to you, but you can control how you respond to it."

From a biblical viewpoint, the same thought can be expressed this way—"God's sovereignty determines *what* we go through; we determine *how* we go through it." It's often our reactions to circumstances that catch people's attention. Do we respond to harsh words with a kind reply or cutting remark? Do we react to selfish actions with equal self-centeredness or unselfish behavior?

If a co-worker is inconsiderate, does your reaction cause her to say, "She's just as bad as I am," or does it cause her to say, "Why didn't she treat me the way I treated her?" The way we react to countless stresses and conflicts of the workplace are evident every day—in conferences, lunchroom conversations, client negotiations, budget planning, service calls, sales meetings, and on the factory line. Every day our reactions are on display.

Do I tell the truth?

Hard work and proper reactions need to be accompanied by truth. When someone says "the truth," we instinctively think about the issue of lying versus telling the truth. Obviously telling the truth is the first and foremost requirement in order to be a truthful person. Truth needs to be seen in sales reports, endorsements, expense reports, budget analyses, client negotiations, and the way we repeat what others say.

But truthfulness runs deeper than appearing honest on the outside. James 5:12 says, "But let your 'Yes' be 'Yes,' and your 'No,' 'No,' lest you fall into judgment." It's the same principle as, "Say what you mean and mean what you say." If you say something as simple as, "I appreciate you" to a co-worker, are you saying it out of honesty or as a way to manipulate the other person? Do you sincerely mean that or are you just trying to make him feel good about you? If you tell a co-worker, "I'll meet you at 8:00," do you mean what you say? Or do you think that if you're there at 8:15, that's close enough? A person once said to me, "I don't mind if someone is going to be fifteen minutes late. What bothers me is when he knows he's going to be late because he's never on time for anything. So why doesn't he give me the actual time?" What we say verbally should be consistent with what we tell ourselves mentally. Say what you mean and mean what you say.

Proverbs 16:13 tells us, "Righteous lips are the delight of kings, and they love him who speaks what is right." Any person in a position of leadership—from king to company president to department manager—values the person who speaks the truth. It should be everyone's delight because it is God's delight. Jesus applied the term "the truth" to Himself (John 14:6). If we want others to deal with us in truth, then we must be certain they see truth as our delight as well.

Do I live consistently?

The question that summarizes all of the issues that we discussed is this: "Am I consistently a good witness?" The emphasis is on the word *consistently.* Do you work as hard one month after your evaluation and pay increase as you did the five months leading up to it? Are Fridays no different than Mondays in terms of work performance? Does everyone get the same Christ-like treatment from you or only those who might help you climb up the ladder? Are your actions as honest when the boss is not looking?

Years ago, the city of Dallas, Texas, honored the legendary coach of the Dallas Cowboys, Tom Landry, with a parade. Thousands turned out to line the streets and cheer for Coach Landry. Anyone who had followed his career knew that he was a committed Christian. Even those who were not Cowboys fans often admired him. One Dallas paper ran a full-page article on the coach, and one comment became the theme of the article: "He was consistent." On the field, off the field, Sunday to Sunday, Coach Landry was consistent in his position as a coach and in his profession as a believer. Consistency should be the flavor of our lives.

What do all these qualities produce? Opportunities. Workplace situations have their limitations. As noted earlier, workers are paid to work, not to witness. We need to be careful not to steal time from our employers. But what can't be said on the job can sometimes be said off the job. What gives us that opportunity is very often a Christian life well lived on the job. As someone has said, "The witness of the life accompanied by the witness of the lips is very powerful."

A man, who for years was antagonistic to Christ, attributed his conversion to a very timid neighbor. Expressing surprise, the neighbor said, "I can't remember that I ever had much to say to you about becoming a Christian." The new believer answered, "No. You didn't have much to say about it but you lived me to death. I could stand their preaching and upset their arguments, but I couldn't stand the way you live."[2]

KEY POINTS

Scripture says to live the life you should. Ask yourself:

- Am I a good worker?
- Do I act and react with self-control?

- Do I tell the truth?
- Do I live consistently?

Answer those questions honestly and make the necessary changes. The results could be life changing, not just for yourself, but also for the people you work with every day.

Part 3

Speak as You Should

*Let your speech always be with grace, seasoned
with salt, that you may know how you ought to
answer each one.*
—Colossians 4:6

Chapter Six

What Does That Mean?

Any helpful book on witnessing in the workplace has to address the instrument that can do the greatest good or the greatest damage—the tongue. It's been said, "The most dangerous animal in the world has its den behind your teeth." Of course, when we use the word *tongue*, we're not talking about just the active muscle in our mouths. It's the verbal communication that takes place, via the tongue, that are the teeth of the beast. This dangerous animal, however, doesn't have to run wild and do nothing but wreak havoc. It can become a means by which we offer the greatest help anyone can offer to another.

Colossians 4:6 says, "Let your speech always be with grace, seasoned with salt, that you may know how you ought to answer each one." Four words or phrases stand out prominently in Paul's admonition to believers.

"Grace"

Our speech should always have a sense of graciousness about it. It should be noted not just for being pleasant but also for conveying acceptance, understanding, and caring. What we say and how we say it can impart a gift to others that is lovely and delightful.

"Salt"

Salt was a helpful analogy for Paul to use in this passage and most likely was brought to mind by the fact that there was a salt lake near the city of Colosse. His readers would have been well aware of the properties of salt. Salt is often used in the Scriptures with one of either two primary characteristics in mind. On the one hand, salt enhances flavor and often makes food tastier. On the other hand, salt acts as a preservative and keeps food edible and wholesome. In the days before refrigeration, salt was the main means of preserving meat in particular.

The analogy of speech with salt gives us a perceptive insight into the kind of speech that should characterize our lives. When we are speaking with grace, seasoned with salt, our words will enhance, not distract, the conversation. We won't be using "distasteful" words. Our speech will have a "wholesomeness" about it that is commendable. The words we say will not only be the right words, but will also be said in the right spirit.

There is also a third action of salt that applies here as well. Salt also creates thirst! When people speak with us, does that interaction leave them wanting to talk with us again? If so, we are truly speaking with the kind of salty graciousness that characterizes a follower of Christ.

"Always"

Always simply means to everyone and at all times. The reason to always speak as Paul advises is simple. You can't change the way you speak when non-Christians are around. The way you speak to people in general will be the way you speak to lost people in particular. If your words are often cutting and critical to believers, there will be times when they'll be cutting and critical to non-Christians. That's why our speech, on a 24-7 basis, needs to be characterized by grace and salt.

We all know the old children's rhyme, "Sticks and stones

may break my bones but words will never hurt me." Most of us have probably used words as a weapon of sorts—a retort to the person who has put us down or ridiculed us. We say words don't hurt, but we use them to do just the opposite—to get back at someone who has verbally hurt us. Words can go beyond hurt. They can wound someone deeply. Even if words don't hurt *you*, they may hurt the person to whom you're speaking. It's therefore wise to choose carefully what you say instead of saying whatever you choose.

"Know How to Answer"

Paul ends his admonition with a special directness—". . . that you may know how you ought to answer each one." The lost person may have completely misunderstood something taught in Scripture. Perhaps he has been turned off by the hypocrisy of another believer. She may be bitter against God because of something God allowed to happen to her. He may be blaming God for something that he should be blaming himself for. Each person is different, and each may need just the right words spoken with just the right spirit in order to move beyond their defensiveness or hurt. Whatever the circumstance, you should speak in a way that moves the person closer to Christ instead of away from Him. Your lips, like your life, should be a help and not a hindrance in communicating Christ to lost people.

So the Bible's guidelines for speaking as we should can be summed up this way: "Cultivate caring and wholesome conversation so you'll know how to answer each person in just the right way." That does not mean we should never confront those who need to be confronted or to be direct with those with whom we have to be direct. It does mean, however, that there's never a need for sarcasm nor a reason to be rude. Instead, our speech, like our life, should work like salt in a person's life. It ought to give them an appetite for God and tantalize them with a wholesomeness so that they desire to know more.

KEY POINTS

"Under improvement" is a phrase that often describes a building being remodeled or a street being resurfaced. It says things are getting better. Proper speech in the workplace is speech that's always getting better—more and more like the speech Christ wants us to use. To improve:

- Be gracious when you talk to others
- Keep the conversation wholesome
- Talk that way with all people at all times
- Speak in a way that moves them closer to Christ

God's charge to us is: "Cultivate caring and wholesome conversation so you'll know how to answer each person in just the right way."

Chapter Seven

How Do We Speak Properly?

The tongue—master or servant? The difference is stark. If it's your master, it controls you. If it's your servant, you control it. How do you make it your servant instead of allowing it to be your master?

Prayer

Controlling how you speak starts where most everything starts—prayer. God gave us the ability to speak but, like all parts of our personalities, speech has been impacted by our own sinful depravity. One of the most vivid descriptions of sin's effect upon what comes out of our mouths is given in Romans 3:13–14:

"Their throat is an open tomb;
With their tongues they have practiced deceit";
"The poison of asps is under their lips";
"Whose mouth is full of cursing and bitterness."

Paul's quotation from several Old Testament passages doesn't paint a pretty picture of the way we speak. Notice that everything gets into the act—the throat, the tongue, the lips, the mouth. All are used as figures of speech to represent the one reality—the words we speak can bring about death, deceit, dysfunction, and destruction.

Psalm 5:9, one of the passages Paul quotes, compares the throat to an "open tomb." It's an example of hyperbole, an exaggerated metaphor that would be funny if it weren't so tragic. Imagine someone whose mouth could open up as wide as a grave opening! Think, however, of how someone's words can be an entrance into the realm of death. Tombs and graves only get opened in order to receive the dead. We use the expression, "If looks could kill," but it's really words that kill, not looks. Lies, slanders, hatred—all spew out of the mouth, propelled by the evil and sin that controls the mind. Think of the horror brought about by someone such as Adolf Hitler, whose mouth became the grave for millions of innocent lives.

Do we ever kill someone with our speech? Have you ever told yourself, "Boy, I really nailed him!"? Our speech can kill someone's spirit, a deadly wound of the soul. We can criticize and demean a person to the point of not only emotional death, but even physical death.

In late 2011, eight soldiers serving in Afghanistan were charged with negligent homicide in the death of one of their fellow soldiers. An investigation revealed that he had been the victim of unrelenting hazing and had been repeatedly taunted with racial slurs. Unable to bear the verbal onslaught any longer, he took his own life.

Paul also quotes Psalm 140:3, which makes an even more deadly comparison between a person's lips and a snake. An "asp" could be one of several venomous snakes that inhabited the Nile region of Egypt, and often was used for the Egyptian cobra—a snake filled with deadly poison. We sometimes say of a dog that "his bark is worse than his bite," but that's never true of a venomous snake. It's never true, either, of words that are intentionally spoken in order to poison a relationship or cutting remarks that "take a bite" out of someone.

Paul also uses a quotation from Psalm 10, which describes a person given over to evil as someone "whose mouth is full of cursing and bitterness." Parents say to a child, "Don't talk when your mouth is full," but this person's mouth is full of the worst words and he won't stop talking. Curses, anger, vengefulness, bitterness all flow out in an endless stream. Not true of us, we think? Just how quick are we to be critical of others? We may be with someone for only a short time, but when that person leaves, we begin to tear him or her down behind their back. Maybe someone mistreated us in the past and we can't let go of our anger. Every opportunity we get, we rehearse our bitterness with anyone who will listen.

Controlling that tongue requires spiritual power, not natural power. It can only be done through Christ. I've seen churches have everything from a building dedication to a baby dedication. I've never seen one have a tongue dedication service—yet I've met more churches that have been destroyed by the tongue than by babies and buildings. Our speech has to be so dedicated to God that we are committed to never use it apart from His direction and to always use it depending on His control. This applies to every area of the workplace, from balancing a budget to building a house. The proper use of our mouths begins by realizing that it can only be used effectively through His power, not through ours. A person once remarked that daily we ought to pray, "God, please keep your arms around my shoulder and your hand across my mouth."

Spiritual Growth

The way we speak is a symptom of where we are spiritually. Spiritually immature people often demonstrate their immaturity by the way they talk. Their mouth leads their mind instead of their mind leading their mouth. Spiritually mature people control the tongue. They don't allow the tongue to control them. As they grow, their Christ-likeness is seen in the way their words are carefully chosen rather than carelessly used.

One example of spiritual maturity is often how few words a person uses, not how many words. Spirituality brings with it wisdom, the wisdom that is God-given. Wise people are noted for how well they listen, not how well they talk. That's the emphasis of Proverbs—wise people listen. In fact, Proverbs goes so far as to say, "Do you see a man hasty in his words? There is more hope for a fool than for him" (Prov. 29:20). We are told, "In the multitude of words sin is not lacking, but he who restrains his lips is wise" (10:19).

With spiritual growth also comes balance. Jesus Christ was noted as a person "full of grace and truth" (John 1:14). There are those who have grace but unfortunately no truth. One person I know often remarked, "Jesus never called anyone a sinner." Nothing could be further from the truth. One example of the way Jesus spoke the truth is found in Matthew 9:13: "For I did not come to call the righteous, but sinners, to repentance." He minced no words in saying to the arrogant Pharisees in John 8:44, "You are of your father the devil."

Then there are those who have truth but no grace. They're quick to tell people they're going to hell and explain why in a very condemning and demeaning way. One wonders while listening to them whether they are sad or glad about the hearer's lost condition. It was a combination of truth and grace that caused Him to say to the woman accused of adultery, "Neither do I condemn you; go and sin no more" (John 8:11). Our lips dare not be characterized by grace without truth or truth without grace. Both are necessary and both are the product of the spiritually balanced believer.

Spiritual growth also brings understanding—understanding that leads to empathy. When are we apt to misuse our tongue the most? When we let others lead us instead of us leading them. They are sarcastic with us, so we get sarcastic with them. They ridicule us, so we ridicule them. They try to outsmart us, so we try to prove we can outsmart them. Spiritually mature people look beyond the person to the problem.

The problem non-Christians have is described in Ephesians 2:1–2: "And you He made alive, who were dead in trespasses and sins, in which you once walked according to the course of this world, according to the prince of the power of the air, the spirit who now works in the sons of disobedience." Simply put, non-Christians are slaves to Satan. Whatever he tells them to do, they are under his orders. Recognizing that fact makes a spiritually mature person feel compassion for them—a response far more effective than getting mad at them. We recognize that our relationship with Christ has set us free from the power of Satan. "Therefore if the Son makes you free, you shall be free indeed" (John 8:36). When Satan tempts us to use our tongue in a demeaning way, we have the authority and power of Christ to say, "No!"

Non-Christians lack the freedom and power that the believer has in Christ. That reality should lead us to pray for them and extend compassion toward them. It's the same empathy for others that was expressed by Jesus in Matthew 9:36 which says, "But when He saw the multitudes, He was moved with compassion for them, because they were weary and scattered, like sheep having no shepherd."

The spiritual depth that produces understanding that leads to compassion will make an impact in the lives of others. Recognizing a person's lost condition, we can respond in our privileged condition—a condition in which the tongue has been freed up to speak rightly, not wrongly.

KEY POINTS

The psalmist prayed, "Let the words of my mouth and the meditation of my heart be acceptable in Your sight, O LORD, my strength and my Redeemer" (Ps. 19:14). Words acceptable to God become words used in the workplace. They are developed through:

- Prayer
- Spiritual growth

Spiritual growth, in turn, produces

- Wisdom
- Balance between grace and truth
- An understanding that leads to compassion for unbelievers

The most dangerous animal in the world has its den behind your teeth. Through the Holy Spirit, master that animal in such a way that it is constructive, not destructive.

Part 4

Know What's Essential

Chapter Eight

What Is "Sin" and How Do We Explain It to a Non-Christian?

The truth is that sin is often enjoyable. A young boy prayed, "Lord, if you can't make me a better boy, don't worry about it. I'm having a good time as it is."[1] Enjoyable as it may be, sin is deadly, so deadly it will send a person to an eternal hell. Unless a person understands sin's consequences, he or she may never see their need for Christ.

Evangelist D. L. Moody once was visiting inmates in a prison and asked each prisoner the same question: "What brought you here?" He received replies such as, "I don't deserve to be here," "I was framed," "I was falsely accused," or "I was given an unfair trial." Not one would admit his guilt. Finally, Moody came to a man with his face buried in his hands, weeping. Moody asked, "What's wrong?" The prisoner answered, "My sins are more than I can bear." Moody responded, "Thank God for that." Moody then had the privilege of introducing him to Christ.[2]

When we come to God, we must come to Him, recognizing that we are sinners. Effectiveness in evangelism therefore demands that we understand the issue of sin and how to explain it to a non-Christian.

Why don't people see themselves as sinners?

What prevents non-Christians from seeing themselves as sinners? There are undoubtedly many answers to this question, but two are paramount. One is pride. Pride makes us focus on what we've done right (or what we think we've done right!) instead of what we've done wrong. The story is told that a university once asked each person applying for admission to complete a personal data sheet. In response to the request to list personal strengths, an eighteen-year-old answered, "Sometimes I am trustworthy, loyal, helpful, friendly, courteous, kind, obedient, cheerful, thrifty, brave, clean, and reverent." When the same form requested a list of personal weaknesses, the same applicant wrote, "Sometimes I am NOT trustworthy, loyal, helpful, friendly, courteous, kind, obedient, cheerful, thrifty, brave, clean, and reverent." Our list of weaknesses is at least as long or longer than our list of personal strengths, but we prefer to focus on what we've done right instead of what we've done wrong.

How many times in confronting unbelievers about their sinful condition before God have you received the response, "I've done a lot of things right in my time. The Lord knows I'm trying to do what is right"? Their focus is on what they've done right, not what they've done wrong.

A second problem is comparison. Non-Christians often choose to compare themselves to those who, in their opinion, live worse than they do. They conclude, "I'm not nearly as bad as a lot of people I know" or "At least I'm not as bad as so-and-so." They seldom question whether or not they are using the right standard. They've chosen the standard that they want to use—the one that makes them look better than most. Whatever the standard of comparison they choose, it's always relative. They can always find someone who is worse than them. How do we explain sin to unbelievers in such a way that they see themselves as hopeless before God's absolute standards?

One word of caution—we cannot do the Holy Spirit's work. Seeing ourselves as God sees us is a spiritual issue. First Corinthians

2:14 reminds us, "But the natural man does not receive the things of the Spirit of God, for they are foolishness to him; nor can he know them, because they are spiritually discerned." Therefore, the Holy Spirit has to do His convicting work. One of the things the Holy Spirit convicts us of is sin; particularly the sin of not believing in Christ. In John 16:8–11, Christ, referring to the Holy Spirit, says, "And when He has come, He will convict the world of sin, and of righteousness, and of judgment: of sin, because they do not believe in Me. . . ." Faith in Christ and His payment for sin is the answer to their sin problem. Therefore, the Holy Spirit wants to convict them of their sinful state. Unless the Holy Spirit works, they will never see themselves as sinners.

What does the Bible say about sin? In confronting issues of pride and comparing ourselves with others, God does two things. First, He focuses on His standard, not ours. His standard is not human goodness. If it were, God could grade on a curve, and most of us might be good enough. Instead, God's standard is perfection, the perfection of His own holiness. Compared to the holiness of God, even the most moral, well-behaved person who has ever lived has fallen short of that standard.

The most common word for "sin" in New Testament Greek is the word *hamartia*. It means "missing the mark," in the sense of an arrow that falls short or misses the target. It's the word used in Romans 3:23, "For all have sinned [*hamartia*] and fall short of the glory of God." One lie, one unkind thought, one moment of lust, and we have missed His standard of perfection. In reality, it's not just one sin—we repeatedly miss the mark and fall short of God's moral standards.

Solomon observed in the Old Testament, "For there is not a just man on earth who does good and does not sin" (Eccl. 7:20). He spoke that same truth when he dedicated the temple and stated, "There is no one who does not sin" (1 Kings 8:46). What proof did Solomon offer to substantiate his statement? He warns us to avoid the person who finds pleasure in exposing the shortcomings of others. Why? Because we ourselves have done what we accuse others of doing. Solomon said, "Also do not take to heart everything people say, lest you hear your servant cursing you. For many times, also, your own heart has known that even you have cursed others" (Eccl. 7:21–22). David wrote, "For in Your sight no one living is righteous" (Ps. 143:2). Since God's standard is perfection, no one is righteous in His sight.

Since humans can only observe other people's behavior and listen to their words, they are sometimes fooled into thinking that others are better than they are. We can't see a person's heart, the motivations and intentions behind their actions and words. But God can't be fooled. He doesn't overlook anything or anyone. What does He observe? "The LORD looks down from heaven upon the children of men, to see if there are any who understand, who seek God. They have all turned aside, they have together become corrupt; there is none who does good, no, not one" (Ps. 14:2–3).

We can reach pretty high standards of performance when we want to. You may be familiar with a business management strategy called Six Sigma, which was developed nearly thirty years ago. Basically it called for focusing on removing defects from a business process (like manufacturing) in circumstances where errors cannot be easily tolerated (like making airplanes). Six Sigma's goal was 99.9996 percent error-free output, that is, 3.4 defects per million. Only 3.4 in a million!

That's a pretty high standard for making airplanes, but it's nowhere near good enough when it comes to humans. God's standard is perfection. No one measures up. A non-Christian must therefore be challenged to compare himself or herself to Christ. They cannot use their neighbors, spouses, fellow employees, or respected religious figures. The standard is perfection as seen in the person of Christ Himself.

The second thing God does to confront our pride is point out our rebellion against Him. A common word used in the New Testament to show our rebellion is the Greek word *adikia*, often translated unrighteousness. *Adikia* is used for a number of rebellious acts from immorality to the violation of governmental laws. We are the opposite of who God is. What He says not to do, we do. What He says to do, we don't do. We are stubborn and rebellious.

Few passages in the Bible address our rebellion more clearly or specifically than Romans 1:28–32:

> And even as they did not like to retain God in their knowledge, God gave them over to a debased mind, to do those things which are not fitting; being filled with all unrighteousness, sexual immorality, wickedness, covetousness, maliciousness; full of envy, murder, strife, deceit, evil-mindedness; they are whisperers, backbiters, haters of God, violent, proud, boasters, inventors of evil things, disobedient to parents, undiscerning, untrustworthy, unloving, unforgiving, unmerciful; who, knowing the righteous judgment of God, that those who practice such things are deserving of death, not only do the same but also approve of those who practice them.

What proof does God give?

What does God use to show us that we have missed His standard and have rebelled against him? He uses the law, particularly the Ten Commandments, to show us how we've fallen short. That is one central purpose of the law: "For by the law is the knowledge of sin" (Rom. 3:20).

Review the Ten Commandments as recorded in Exodus 20:1–17. God commands, "You shall not take the name of the LORD your God in vain." Every time we use the name of God in an irreverent or flippant way, we prove that we are sinners. We have missed the mark. God commands, "You shall not bear false witness against your neighbor." Every time we lie about someone, we prove that we are sinners. We have missed the mark. God commands, "You shall not covet your neighbor's house; you shall not covet your neighbor's wife . . . nor anything that is your neighbor's." When we covet what someone else has, we prove that we are sinners. We have missed the mark. The Ten Commandments show us the specifics of how we have fallen short. The law cannot remove our sinful condition, but it does prove our sinful condition. No one can read the Ten Commandments objectively and not conclude, "I have sinned."

So how do we explain that we are all sinners?

The same two ideas that the Scriptures use to prove we are sinners are the same two ideas we should use—missing the mark and rebellion. To explain why we are all sinners, we should use the same standard the New Testament uses, the Ten Commandments. We need to explain that (1) we have missed the mark and (2) we have rebelled against God.

By directing a nonbeliever to the Ten Commandments, we address both the issues of pride and the temptation to compare ourselves with others. We have directed them to God rather than human standards of goodness or perfection. No one measures up. We have all fallen short, whether we have sinned once or one hundred times. God's standard is not the preacher or the pope; God's standard is perfection as seen in Christ alone.

We have also addressed rebellion. What God says not to do, we do. What God says to do, we don't do. Years of speaking to non-Christians have proven to me that one of the best ways to show a non-Christian that he or she is a sinner is to do what the New Testament does—use the law. Through the law, the whole world stands guilty before God (Rom. 3:19). If an unbeliever is familiar with the Ten Commandments, it only takes a moment to explain what they are and why God gave them. Using commandments such as "You shall not take the name of the LORD your God in vain," and "You shall not covet" can make it clear that they are sinners. In fact, they break His commandments every day.

Some may wonder, "Should we mention hell as the ultimate consequence of sin?" We need to feel free to speak about the reality of hell, but we must do it with compassion. If we do not feel a tinge of sorrow that a non-Christian could spend eternity there, we need to ask God to give us that sense of grief. Hell should never be mentioned with a spirit of revenge as though to say, "You'll get what you deserve." It needs to be mentioned with a depth of sorrow that says, "God doesn't want you to go there."

What about those who, when confronted with the Ten Commandments, deny their wrongs or, at best, minimize them? They don't see themselves as rebellious against God.

Once again, it is not for us to do the work of the Holy Spirit. They may attempt to live in denial, but that's all it is—an attempt. They must deal with their own conscience. Romans 2:13–15 speaks to that issue:

> For not the hearers of the law are just in the sight of God, but the doers of the law will be justified; for when Gentiles, who do not have the law, by nature do the things in the law, these, although not having the law, are a law to themselves, who show the work of the law written in their hearts, their conscience also bearing witness, and between themselves their thoughts accusing or else excusing them.

While they can deny their guilt to us, they cannot hide it from themselves.

KEY POINTS

Unless our co-workers see themselves as sinners, they will never see their need of a Savior. Lost people must understand, through the convicting work of the Holy Spirit that:

- Sin is missing the mark
- Sin is rebellion
- The Ten Commandments tell us that we are guilty of both

Once we understand the depth of our need, it is then we are positioned to understand the depth of His grace.

Chapter Nine

What Is Our Message
for Non-Christians?

It's been said, "The better you know what you're talking about, the more simply you can put it." God wants us to keep our message to non-Christians simple and understandable. To do so, we need to know what our message is.

You may ask, "Isn't our message to non-Christians the gospel?" After all, Mark 16:15 tells us, "Go into all the world and preach the gospel to every creature."

Most certainly our message is the gospel. But what is the gospel? Evangelist D. L. Moody once said, "I do not think there is a word in the English language so little understood as the word 'gospel.'"[1] As a test, ask a group of believers the question, "What is the gospel?" and note the variety of answers you'll most likely get. If Christians are confused about the gospel, how will the nonbeliever ever understand our message?

Why is there confusion?

There are a number of reasons for this confusion. For starters, the word *gospel* is sometimes used as a generic term to refer to any truth. "I'm telling you the gospel truth" may refer to a statement made about a friend, the weather forecast, a hard-to-believe fact, or a promise we intend to keep. Sometimes it is used as a synonym for the entire Bible. Hence Genesis to Revelation and creation to end-time events are all considered the gospel. In Christian circles, the first four books of the New Testament are traditionally referred to as the "Gospels" of Matthew, Mark, Luke, and John. Finally, Christians sometimes refer to the gospel by using the English translation "good news." They may say that the "good news" is that God loves us. While it is true that God loves us, that alone is not the gospel that is truly good news.

When Jesus told His disciples, "Go into all the world and preach the gospel to every creature" (Mark 16:15), He was referring to a very specific truth. Paul referred to it as "the gospel of the grace of God." He wrote, "But none of these things move me; nor do I count my life dear to myself, so that I may finish my race with joy, and the ministry which I received from the Lord Jesus, to testify to the gospel of the grace of God" (Acts 20:24).

How does God define the gospel?

The historical elements and meaning of the gospel are most clearly defined in the Scriptures in 1 Corinthians 15:3–5. What adds weight to Paul's definition of the gospel is that the gospel he defined came straight from God to him and then to the Corinthians. In verse 3 Paul wrote, "For I delivered to you [the Corinthian believers] first of all that which I also received." "Received" is the same word Paul used in Galatians 1:12 where he said, "For I neither received it [the gospel] from man, nor was I taught it, but it came through the revelation of Jesus Christ." The gospel Paul received and declared was not the result of a church council decision or a product of his own imagination. Its origin was of God.

What is the message that Paul received? "That Christ died for our sins according to the Scriptures, and that He was buried, and that He rose again the third day according to the Scriptures, and that He was seen by Cephas, then by the twelve" (1 Cor. 15:3–5). Paul's definition of the gospel centers around four main verbs:

- Christ <u>died</u> for our sins according to the Scriptures.
- He was <u>buried</u>.
- He <u>rose</u> again the third day according to the Scriptures.
- He <u>was seen</u>.

Let's look at those four verbs in more detail.

"Christ <u>died</u> for our sins." While we as Christians take it for granted that Jesus actually died on the cross, within a few generations of the first century, various heretical groups would deny that Jesus had actually died. Some denied that Jesus was fully human, and therefore, as a spirit being, could not experience death. One group, the Gnostics, separated the man Jesus from the divine being, Christ. The Gnostics proposed that it was Christ who descended on Jesus at His baptism but left Jesus before His death on the cross.[2] So, first of all, we believe that Jesus physically died on the cross. The preposition used here by Paul, however, gives us an even more important truth to share. "For" is the translation of a Greek preposition that means "instead of" or "on behalf of." Jesus didn't just die as an example of sacrificial love for others. He died in our place as our substitute. The death we deserved for our sins, Jesus took in our place.

The story is told of a man who took his young son fishing but unfortunately only brought along one life jacket. A storm came up and strong winds capsized the boat. The father put the vest on his son and pushed him toward shore. The last words the son heard his dad say were "I love you." The father died in the son's place. Had the father not died, the son would have. The father saved his son by dying for him. In a similar way Jesus Christ took our place. He was hung on the cross where we should have hung. He died as the substitute for our sins.

"According to the Scriptures" tells us that His death was the fulfillment of what was prophesied seven hundred years earlier when the prophet Isaiah wrote, "But He was wounded for our transgressions, He was bruised for our iniquities" (Isa. 53:5).

Second, Paul notes that "He <u>was buried</u>." Why mention this? His burial is irrefutable proof that He actually died. Jesus didn't just appear to die—He actually died, and His body was placed in a tomb. With the rise of Islam almost seven hundred years after Jesus, Muslim teaching denied that Jesus died and was buried as the Scriptures state. The Qur'an accords Jesus the status of a prophet, but not a Savior who died for our sins. According to the Qur'an, God couldn't allow His prophet to die a shameful death, so at the last minute, God miraculously substituted the form of another person for Jesus on the cross. Some Muslims believe that it was Judas who was substituted for Jesus. The bottom line is that in Islamic teaching, Jesus did not die on the cross and was not buried in a tomb.[3] The truth of the gospel is that Jesus died for our sins and was buried, which proves the reality of His death.

"He <u>rose</u> again the third day according to the Scriptures." Christ's resurrection, just like His crucifixion, was prophesied hundreds of years earlier. David predicted the resurrection of Christ when he wrote in Psalm 16:10, "For You will not leave my soul in Sheol, nor will You allow Your Holy One to see corruption." It is this passage that the apostle Peter quotes on the Day of Pentecost when the first public proclamation of Jesus' resurrection is made to the multitude of listeners who gathered around the disciples. Peter said:

> Men and brethren, let me speak freely to you of the patriarch David, that he is both dead and buried, and his tomb is with us to this day. Therefore, being a prophet, and knowing that God had sworn with an oath to him that of the fruit of his body, according to the flesh, He would raise up the Christ to sit on his throne, he, foreseeing this, spoke concerning the resurrection of the Christ, that His soul was not left in Hades, nor did His flesh see corruption. This Jesus God has raised up. (Acts 2:29–32)

Death did not conquer Jesus. Jesus conquered death! The power of death has been broken by the power of God!

"He <u>was seen</u>." Just as Paul mentioned Christ's burial as proof that He died, he mentions the fact that He was seen as proof He arose. One of the strongest types of evidence in a courtroom is the consistent agreement of multiple eyewitnesses. In essence, Paul lays out the legal evidence and gives a list of the witnesses who can testify:

> He was seen by Cephas, then by the twelve. After that He was seen by over five hundred brethren at once, of whom the greater part remain [are alive] to the present, but some have fallen asleep. After that He was seen by James, then by all the apostles. Then last of all He was seen by me also, as by one born out of due time. For I am the least of the apostles, who am not worthy to be called an apostle, because I persecuted the church of God. (1 Cor. 15:5–9)

These were not people prone to hallucinations, nor were these uninformed witnesses who did not know Christ and could have mistaken Him for someone else. The Person they saw was real, and they actually knew Him.

As the final witness, Paul lists himself and adds a noteworthy fact: of all the witnesses, Paul would have been the *least* likely to accept the fact of the resurrection. Paul was not initially a follower of Christ; instead, he forcefully persecuted believers, arresting them and throwing them into prison. That such a person could be convinced of the resurrection is powerful testimony indeed!

His burial is proof of His death. The fact that Jesus was seen is proof of His resurrection. So simply stated the gospel is: Christ died for our sins and rose from the dead. Ten words stated so simply that even the newest convert can share with a friend. The Bible contains sixty-six books and can never be fully grasped in a lifetime. The gospel can be stated in ten words and can be learned in a minute—Christ died for our sins and rose from the dead.

What are the ramifications of the gospel?

Looking at this definition more closely, we discover that the gospel has several ramifications. For one, it concerns something

Christ has done. It is past, proven, and completed. The gospel is not about something God will do in our life. It is about something He has already done—more than two thousand years ago. There are many things God can do in a person's life—bring contentment, provide inner peace, and give a purpose for living. But they are not the gospel. The gospel concerns what has already been done for us—Christ died for our sins and rose from the dead.

The gospel also focuses on our relationship with God, not our relationship with others. God can reconcile marriages and help a couple that walked the aisle together to also walk through life together. He can restore relationships in such a way that enemies become friends. These examples concern horizontal relationships; the gospel deals with our vertical relationship. Our primary problem is not that we are separated from one another. Our problem, first and foremost, is our lack of a relationship with God. Christ's death for our sins destroyed the enmity between God and us and makes possible a way whereby we could be His friends. He did for us what we could not do for ourselves. "Christ died for our sins" means that if we trust what He did for us, we can have a relationship with God and ultimately be with Him rather than separated from Him.

The gospel's emphasis is also upon eternal life, not temporal life. That is why a clear understanding of the gospel message is needed in every culture. A person in India who comes to Christ may still die of leprosy. A new believer in Ethiopia may still die of starvation. An African Christian may still suffer from AIDS. An American who comes to Christ may still lose his job or suffer a marital breakup. The gospel, however, centers on life in the hereafter. Its emphasis is on eternal life with God. That eternal life begins the day a person trusts Christ, and it continues forever in His presence.

That "good news" of the gospel is first of all good because Jesus died for our sins, making forgiveness and reconciliation to God possible. It's also good news because He rose from the dead, demonstrating that He is the Son of God who indeed has conquered death. This good news leaves a non-Christian without any excuse for not trusting Christ. Someone may doubt God's love because of the sudden death of a relative or friend, a prolonged hardship, or personal illness. If a person questions God's love, however, he or she must start with the cross. The fact that Jesus died for us removes any and all questions about God's love. He did for us what we would never do for ourselves or for another. Romans 5:7–8 aptly declares, "For scarcely for a righteous man will one die; yet perhaps for a good man someone would even dare to die. But God demonstrates His own love toward us, in that while we were still sinners, Christ died for us."

If an unbeliever doubts that Jesus Christ is God, all he has to do is go back to the empty tomb. The resurrection of Christ has been declared by many to be the most attested fact of history. John Singleton Copley, one of the great legal minds in British history and three-time High Chancellor of England, wrote, "I know pretty well what evidence is, and I tell you, such evidence as that for His resurrection has never broken down yet."[4] There are thousands of references in secular history to that resurrection. Dr. Donald G. Barnhouse noted, "The angel rolled away the stone from Jesus' tomb, not to let the living Lord out, but to let unconvinced outsiders in."[5] What makes that resurrection so important? The bodily resurrection of Jesus Christ from the dead is the crowning proof of Christianity.[6] His resurrection the third day proved His victory over sin and the grave.

So how does the gospel impact our evangelism?

As someone has said, "The main thing is to make the main thing the main thing." What is our message for unbelievers? It's the gospel. Christ died for our sins and rose from the dead. No matter whom we speak to in the workplace or where we speak to them, the gospel is our message for them. Christ died for our sins and rose from the dead.

Making the substitutionary death and His resurrection clear to non-Christians is a moral issue before God. That message is so near and dear to God's heart that Paul even said, as he was inspired by the Holy Spirit, "But even if we, or an angel from heaven, preach any other gospel to you than what we have preached to you, let him be accursed" (Gal. 1:8). It is the one area where we must not speak with confusion. When it comes to the gospel, we must be clear, be clear, be clear! The better we understand our message, the more simply we can state it.

KEY POINTS

We dare not speak confusingly where God speaks clearly. Our message is the gospel (1 Cor. 15:3–5).

The gospel centers around four verb phrases:

- Christ died, He was buried (that is the proof that He died)
- He rose again, He was seen (that is the proof that He rose)

The gospel is contained in ten words—Christ died for our sins and rose from the dead. For the sake of Christ and for the sake of the lost, be clear, be clear, be clear!

Chapter Ten

What Does the Bible Mean by "Believe"?

irections are critical. Without them, there is no way to arrive at a particular destination. I read a humorous story in which torrential rainstorms knocked down power lines all over town. A customer service representative dispatched repairmen to numerous residences. One lineman called to get a customer's exact address and directions. He was told, "I'm at post office box 99." The weary lineman replied, "Ma'am, I'll be coming to you in a truck, not an envelope."[1]

Directions to God are simple. There is only one way. We come through Christ. His words were unmistakably clear: "I am the way, the truth, and the life. No one comes to the Father, except through Me" (John 14:6). The question is, "How do we get to Christ?"

The answer is "believe," a word used ninety-eight times in the gospel of John, the one book specifically written to tell us how to receive eternal life (cf. John 20:31). John 3:36 expresses John's recurring theme, "He who believes in the Son has everlasting life." But what does "believe" mean?

Confusion often surrounds word choices. Take the word *box*. To some it's an object. To others, it's an activity. Adults might think of a cardboard container that holds winter clothing for half the year and summer clothing the other half. Children might think of a four by six structure in the backyard that contains sand and muddied toys. An athlete will probably think of raising his fists before an opponent and driving home a knockout punch. Our life experiences often conjure up what we mean by the word *box*.

Let's take another word—*pad*. A cook thinks of the item he places underneath a hot pan to keep it from scorching the table. A pet lover thinks of a soft rug his pet sleeps on. An NFL player thinks of the cushion underneath his jersey that protects him from the hard blows of the opposing team. In the 1960s a "pad" was where someone lived! Once again, our life experiences conjure up the meaning of *pad* for us.

The word *believe* presents similar problems that can lead to confusion. To some, *believe* means nothing more than hope or speculation:

> "I believe I can be there by five o'clock."
> "I believe I know how to find your house."
> "I believe I laid it on the top shelf of the guest room closet."
> "I believe you are better at that than I am."

To others, *believe* is an intellectual assent to a set of facts.

> "I believe that advertisement is right—that company makes the best passenger truck on the market."
> "I believe that store has better customer service than their competitor. I know because I shop there regularly."
> "I believe what he said. He has never lied to me."

So what does the Bible mean by "believe"?

Believe means "to accept as true."

When we look in a Greek lexicon for the word *pisteuo* (believe), it would say, "be convinced of something, give credence to." We must be convinced that it is a historical fact that more than two thousand years ago Jesus Christ died on a cross and rose the third day. History proves it. The cross and the empty tomb are two of the most attested facts of history. But reading those facts is not enough. We must accept them as being true.

Note that we are not merely accepting as true that Christ died and arose from the dead. We are acknowledging that He did it for us. It was a substitutionary ("instead of us") death. He did not die to show us how to love each other enough to die for each other. Nor did He die to show us how to die sacrificially, without revenge or hatred. Instead, He died in our place. The nails that should have been driven through our hands and feet were driven through His.

Outdoor Life magazine once told of a thirty-six-year-old mother who, along with her three children, was horseback riding in the Similkameen backcountry, thirty miles northwest of Princeton, British Columbia. All four felt a mixture of excitement and freedom as they traveled the vast wilderness. As they were headed to a cabin where they would join the rest of the family for a camping vacation, the horses became increasingly nervous. It became clear why. A cougar suddenly jumped from the undergrowth at Steve, the six-year-old son. The cougar soon had the child in a clawed death grip. The mother, a knowledgeable outdoorswoman, knew her son would be dead in seconds from a broken neck or crushed artery. She leaped from her horse and with adrenaline-fueled strength broke off a limb from a nearby tree and clubbed the cat away from her little boy.

Now the lion turned his attention on her, opening a terrible gash in her arm with one blow. The mother screamed for the older children to pick up the bleeding son and run to the campground for help. An hour later, help returned. The mother's question as she continued to resist the cougar was, "Are my children all right?" On hearing they were okay, she whispered, "I am dying now." The rescuers shot the cougar and rushed to the mother's aid, but she was beyond help. She traded her life for that of her son who survived. She was awarded the Star of Courage posthumously by the governor general of Canada.[2]

Christ died in our place. He suffered the punishment we should have received. He became our substitute. Christ saved us by dying for us. The third day He arose, proving that He had conquered both sin and the grave.

Believe means "to trust."

Ask some people, particularly ones from a religious background, "Do you believe Christ died for you and rose again?" They may answer, "Yes." At the same time, they might express a conviction that without being baptized one cannot be saved. The problem is—they are not "believing" in the biblical sense of the word. Once again, let's consult a Greek lexicon and look up the word *pisteuo* (believe). Along with "be convinced of something, give credence to," we will find "trust." If we believe in the biblical sense of the word, then we are trusting Christ to save us—not our good life, church attendance, baptism, taking of the sacraments, or keeping of the commandments.

No better word brings out the meaning of "believe" to a twenty-first century audience than the word *trust*. We must be sensitive to the fact that some people believe in Christ in the sense that they accept Him as a historical figure who died and arose, but they are not trusting Him to save them, which is what the biblical word *believe* involves.

Several years ago I flew to Washington, DC, to speak at a graduate school. En route, I had the opportunity to speak to an associate pastor of a church in the DC area. As we talked about spiritual things, I said, "Let me ask you the test question. If you stood before God, and He were to ask, 'Why should I let you into heaven?' what would you tell Him?" He answered, "All I'd say is, the blood of Jesus Christ." As we talked, it was clear that he understood that eternal life was free and had trusted Christ to save him.

I then explained why I had asked—I don't take anyone's salvation for granted. He answered, "I certainly understand." He then told me of a preacher in his denomination that had been invited to speak at their church. As the church leadership talked with him, they realized he was not certain he was going to heaven. So they asked him, "Do you know for sure you're going to heaven?" The preacher said, "Of course not. No one can know that." As they continued questioning him, it became obvious he did not understand that eternal life was a gift. He even became defensive about his personal salvation. He believed Christ died and arose but had not trusted Christ to save him.

The easiest way to help a person to understand what it means to believe is by using the word *trust*. I've often said, after discussing spiritual issues with a nonbeliever, "I think you do believe. You believe Jesus Christ was a historical figure who died on a cross and arose, and you even feel He did it for you. But I think you are trusting in your good life to save you." Repeatedly, people have responded, "Oh, you're right." I then explain, "But that's what I want you to understand. *Believe*, in the Bible, means you must trust in Christ alone to save you." As we evangelize, we must consistently ask, "Are you trusting in Christ alone to save you?" Use the word *trust*.

For years I have cautioned believers not to use the following phrases in one-to-one evangelism. I encourage speakers as well (an opportunity that will be addressed later) not to use them in evangelistic speaking.

"Invite Jesus into your heart."

First of all, the Bible does not use this phrase for trusting Christ. Some people point to Revelation 3:20 to support this concept, but this verse is addressed to believers, not unbelievers. It says, "Behold, I stand at the door and knock. If anyone hears My voice and opens the door, I will come in to him and dine with him, and he with Me." Why does this apply to believers and not to unbelievers?

It's important to note the immediate context in verse 19: "As many as I love, I rebuke and chasten." *Chasten* means child training, an indication that He is speaking to believers—those who are already children of God. The Greek preposition translated "in to" in Revelation 3:20 actually means "toward." Jesus is using figurative language to say to Christians that He will "enter the church and come toward the believer" for fellowship. Finally, "dine" referred to the main meal of the day to which someone invited an honored guest. It was the meal given to hospitality and conversation. The offer is one of intimate fellowship, not entrance into a relationship.

When we speak about the gospel to a nonbeliever, the issue is not inviting Jesus into one's heart, but trusting Christ alone to save. Once we trust Christ, He lives within us. There is no need to invite Him in.

"Give your life (or heart) to God."

This is also not a phrase the Bible uses for trusting Christ. The issue is not giving Him one's life or heart. Rather He gives us His life. First John 5:11 tells us, "And this is the testimony: that God has given us eternal life, and *this life is in His Son*" (italics mine). There is nothing eternal about your life. When you trust Christ, you begin to live forever because you have His life inside of you.

"Would you like to pray to receive Christ?"

Again, this is not a phrase that the Bible uses either. The issue is not saying a prayer—it's trusting Christ. Prayer may be how you tell God what you are doing, but saying a prayer does not save anyone. It's trusting Christ that saves. I've often encouraged people that I've led to Christ to pray and tell God what they are doing. I have found that verbalizing it to God helps them verbalize it to others. But I always caution them, "It's not the prayer that saves; it's trusting Christ that saves."

"Accept Christ."

This phrase is so open to interpretation and can mislead a person completely. An unbeliever may accept Christ the way we accept one another—as a person. He may accept Christ as a person who historically lived and died, and yet not trust in Christ to save him. Sometimes a person may refer to John 1:12 to support the idea of accepting Christ. That verse reads, "But as many as received Him, to them He gave the right to become children of God, *to those who believe* in His name" (italics mine). It's important to note what the verse says: "receiving Him" means "to believe." Once again, use the word *trust*.

To *believe* means to trust in Christ alone.

Trusting Christ saves. But inherent in trusting Christ is a third idea. We must trust in Christ *alone* to save us.

What were Christ's last words from the cross? "It is finished" (John 19:30). "Finished" is the translation of the Greek word *tetelestai*, which means "paid in full." Receipts for taxes during New Testament times have been recovered with the word *tetelestai* written across them, meaning "paid in full." Jesus Christ did not make the down payment for our sins to God. He made the full payment.

Therefore, a person is only saved when he is trusting Christ alone to save him—not Christ plus something, such as good works or church attendance, but Christ alone. The message behind the gospel is that we must be satisfied with the thing that satisfies God. If we are satisfied with Christ and our church attendance to give us a right standing with God, we have not truly trusted in Christ.

Suppose we ignore Christ's substitutionary death and resurrection and depend on a life of good works to save us. Or suppose we depend on Christ's substitutionary death and resurrection *and* our good works to save us. Have we disregarded what Christ did on our behalf? Yes, in both instances. Unless we believe Christ alone saves, we have not accepted as true Christ's declaration, "It is finished." We have not trusted Christ.

I have often used three circles to help people understand that Christ alone saves. Inside one circle I put a "W" to represent the good works they've done, whether it be going to church, living a good life, being baptized, loving one's neighbor, etc. Inside the middle circle, I put "C+W" for Christ plus works. Inside the third circle I put "C" for Christ alone. So the three circles look like this.

Then I explain, "There are some people who trust in works to save them (the good things they've done), some who trust in Christ plus works, and some who trust in Christ alone. Where are you?" It's alarming how many people point to "C+W."

Then I explain:

1. If you're trusting in good works to get you to heaven, you're saying Christ's death was unnecessary (I write the word "unnecessary" below the left circle). If anything you can do gets you to heaven, there was no need for Christ to die. In fact, if anything we did gets us to heaven, God made a fool out of His own Son because there was no need for Him to die.

2. If you are trusting Christ-plus-works, you are saying His death was disappointing. He paid for some sins; I have to pay for others. He didn't get the job done. He disappointed God; He disappointed me (I write the word "disappointing" below the middle circle).

3. If you are trusting Christ alone, you are saying His death is sufficient. (I write the word "sufficient" underneath the right circle.) I then direct them to Christ's words in John 19:30, "It is finished."

So now the circles look like this:

Unnecessary   Disappointing   Sufficient

I sincerely do not know how many people have been led to Christ using these three circles to communicate the sufficiency of Christ's death for our sins.

As we evangelize, we must explain that God asks us to trust in

Christ alone to save us. Only when we are trusting Christ alone to save us are we satisfied with the thing that satisfies God. To believe in the biblical sense of the word is to trust in Christ alone as our only way to heaven.

KEY POINTS

The directions that we give to people on how to come to Christ are the most critical of all directions. In inviting unbelievers to come to Christ, we must:

- Explain to them that they must come to God as sinners, recognize Christ died for them and rose again, and trust in Christ alone to save them
- Not use phrases that confuse non-Christians
- Be certain they understand that they are trusting Christ PERIOD, not Christ PLUS anything they have done

Upon trusting Christ alone as their only way to heaven, their only way to a right relationship with God, then and only then do they have eternal life through faith in Christ.

Chapter Eleven

Where Does Repentance Fit In?

An evangelistic speaker posed the question, "How do you come to Christ?" He then gave the audience his answer—"You begin with repentance. You recognize you've been going the wrong direction. You make an about face and decide to follow Christ. You then have to accept Him as your Lord and Savior. You have to let Him control all your thoughts and decisions. Unless you repent, you cannot come to Christ."

Several things are interesting about his answer. One is the fact that changing the direction of one's life preceded coming to Christ. Second, only when a person changed the direction of his or her life could that person come to Christ. Third, in coming to Christ a person had to be willing to give Him complete control of his or her life. The fourth thing to observe, however, is that nowhere was any comment made as to the freeness of salvation. He made no mention of the fact that we are accepted by God not based on what we've done for Him, but based on what He's done for us. A fifth observation is perhaps the most striking of all: nowhere did he ask the audience to do what the gospel of John asks people to do—believe.

His entire answer was wrapped around the idea of repentance. Is repentance essential to salvation? What part does repentance play in salvation? As we evangelize, it is essential that we have a biblical understanding of repentance.

Repentance is essential to salvation.

We know from such clear statements as Acts 17:30–31 that repentance is essential to salvation. In that passage we read, "Truly, these times of ignorance God overlooked, but now commands all men everywhere to repent, because He has appointed a day on which He will judge the world in righteousness by the Man whom He has ordained. He has given assurance of this to all by raising Him from the dead." As Paul spoke to the people of Athens on Mars Hill, he placed their gods against his—idols of stone against the resurrected Christ. Instead of thinking of God as something they had created, they had to recognize God as the One who created them. Since God would judge the whole world by His Son, people everywhere are commanded to repent.

Consider 2 Peter 3:9. In responding to questions raised about the promise of the Lord's return to some who were becoming disgruntled, Peter explained, "The Lord is not slack concerning His promise, as some count slackness, but is longsuffering toward us, not willing that any should perish but that all should come to repentance." Note again the emphasis on "all." Repentance is seen not as something we might do, but as something we must do. Repentance is essential to salvation.

Repentance implies faith or is associated with faith.

In the gospel of John, the author writes to tell us how to receive eternal life (John 20:31). Ninety-eight times the word *believe* is used. The most familiar verse of that book says, "For God so loved the world that He gave His only begotten Son, that whoever believes in Him should not perish but have everlasting life" (3:16). How many times in the gospel of John is the word *repent* used? Not once. Therefore, we can safely conclude that when used in a salvation context, repentance either implies faith or is associated with faith.

In Acts 10:43 Peter is speaking to Cornelius, a God-fearing Gentile about Jesus: "To Him all the prophets witness that, through His name, whoever believes in Him will receive remission of sins."

Peter clearly understood that belief in Christ was the sole requirement for an eternal right standing with God. Yet, as we have seen above in 2 Peter 3:9, he also stressed the need to repent.

Paul likewise understood that faith or belief was the sole condition of a right standing with God. He stated in Acts 13:39, "And by Him everyone who believes is justified from all things from which you could not be justified by the law of Moses." Four chapters later, though, he stresses the need for "all men everywhere to repent" (17:30).

Repentance either implies faith or is associated with faith. That would explain why, when used in a salvation context, repentance includes believing and at other times it's distinct from believing. In Mark 1:15 we read, "The time is fulfilled, and the kingdom of God is at hand. Repent, and believe in the gospel." That would also explain why it is only used once in the epistle to the Romans. Romans 2:4 reads, "Or do you despise the riches of His goodness, forbearance, and longsuffering, not knowing that the goodness of God leads you to repentance?"

Lewis Sperry Chafer makes the astute observation that "in like manner, the Gospel of John, which is written to present Christ as the object of faith unto eternal life, does not once employ the word *repentance*. Similarly, the Epistle to the Romans, which is the complete analysis of all that enters into the whole plan of salvation by grace, does not use the word *repentance* in connection with the saving of a soul, except in 2:4 where repentance is equivalent to salvation itself."[1]

When used in a salvation context, to repent is to believe in Christ. That's why we do not need to apologize for not using the word *repentance* when talking to people about their salvation. When we call upon a non-Christian audience to trust Christ, we have called upon them to repent. We have called upon them to do what the gospel of John asks—believe.

Repentance means to change your mind, not your life.

The two principal Greek works in the New Testament for "repentance" and "repent" are *metanoia* and *metanoeo*.[2] The basic meaning of the terms is "a change of mind" or "to change one's mind." When the object of repentance is stated, the verb form has one of five objects: God (Acts 20:21), idols (Rev. 9:20), particular sins (9:21), deeds (16:11), and dead works (Heb. 6:1). When the object is implied, it is often Christ, as in Acts 2:38: "Then Peter said to them, 'Repent, and let every one of you be baptized in the name of Jesus Christ for the remission of sins; and you shall receive the gift of the Holy Spirit.'"

It is evident from these passages that a particular change of mind is involved—a change of mind regarding Christ, idolatry, specific sins, deeds, or the inability of one's good works to save oneself. William Evans makes this helpful comment:

> Thus, when Peter, on the Day of Pentecost, called upon the Jews to repent (Acts 2:14–40), he virtually called upon them to change their minds and their views regarding Christ. They had considered Christ to be a mere man, a blasphemer, an imposter. The events of the few preceding days had proven to them that He was none other than the righteous Son of God, their Saviour and the Saviour of the world. The result of their repentance or change of mind would be that they would receive Jesus Christ as their long promised Messiah.[3]

Raised in a religious home, I was of the opinion that my good living, honesty, church attendance, and baptism would save me. As I studied the Scriptures, it became clear to me that eternal life was a gift. Good works or religious efforts could not earn it. Dropping to my knees by my bed as a young person, I changed my mind. I repented about my thinking that my good works would save me, and I trusted Christ as my only way to heaven.

Those who would define repentance as changing one's life often cite Acts 26:20 as proof that repentance is something additional to faith. This passage states that Paul "declared first to those in Damascus and in Jerusalem, and throughout all the region of Judea, and then to the Gentiles, that they should repent, turn to God, and do works befitting repentance." They maintain that this passage teaches that a person must "turn" and then bring forth or produce "works befitting repentance."

Two observations need to be made. First, the context makes it clear that repentance is changing one's mind concerning the person and work of Christ. Repentance in the context of Acts 26, as in other passages, does not speak to the issue of changing one's life, but instead to changing one's mind, believing that Christ is indeed the promised Messiah. Two verses later we read, "Therefore, having obtained help from God, to this day I stand, witnessing both to small and great, saying no other things than those which the prophets and Moses said would come—that the Christ would suffer, that He would be the first to rise from the dead, and would proclaim light to the Jewish people and to the Gentiles" (Acts 26:22–23).

Second, the Greek word translated "befitting" means "corresponding to" or "worthy of." They were to do works that demonstrated how appreciative they were of their salvation. But to handle the text properly, one cannot make fruit a condition so as to say, "No fruit means no repentance." More than one believer in the New Testament did not always live a worthy life, but both the text and context make clear that indeed they were believers.

Changing one's life is not the issue and understandably so. God offers His gift with no strings attached. John 6:47 says, "He who believes in Me has everlasting life." To make the issue changing one's life is not only an unbiblical presentation of the gospel, it confuses salvation (entering the Christian life) with sanctification (living the Christian life). First one enters the Christian life through simple trust in Christ. When we come to God as sinners, recognizing that Christ died for our sins and arose from the dead, and trust in Christ alone to save us, both faith and repentance have taken place. We are entirely His. We then live the Christian life by walking in obedience to Him. Our salvation, though, is never conditioned on that obedience.

When we say, "You must come to Christ, accepting Him as Lord," that is only biblical if we mean that we must acknowledge the fact that He is the Lord God Almighty. But if we mean that we must make Him Lord of every area of our lives, we have confused salvation and sanctification. Making Him Lord of every area of our life, that is, surrendering our self-will to His will, is part of growing as a disciple. It has nothing to do with salvation.

We cannot change our life before coming to Christ in order to be accepted by Him. The grip of sin and temptation is so strong that apart from Him, there is no victory. Only after coming to Him and relying upon Him and His indwelling strength day by day can we say "no" to sin and "yes" to a life of righteousness. That's why Paul says, "And do not present your members as instruments of unrighteousness to sin, but present yourselves to God as being alive from the dead, and your members as instruments of righteousness to God. For sin shall not have dominion over you, for you are not under law but under grace" (Rom. 6:13–14). God never says, "Clean up your life and come to Me." God says, "Come to Me." It is through coming to Him that He helps us clean up our lives by taking out of our lives what should not be there and putting in what should be there.

So repentance, as it relates to salvation, could be defined as "to change your mind about what is keeping you from trusting Christ and trusting Him alone to save you." Once we have trusted Christ, both repentance and faith have taken place.

Tears are not the issue.

The confusion surrounding repentance also relates to the shedding of tears. Some teach that if there are no tears, there is no repentance because there is no sorrow for one's sin.

Some have incorrectly understood 2 Corinthians 7:8–10, in which Paul says:

> For even if I made you sorry with my letter, I do not regret it; though I did regret it. For I perceive that the same epistle made you sorry, though only for a while. Now I rejoice, not that you were made sorry, but that your sorrow led to

repentance. For you were made sorry in a godly manner, that you might suffer loss from us in nothing. For godly sorrow produces repentance leading to salvation, not to be regretted; but the sorrow of the world produces death.

In this passage Paul was not speaking to believers about salvation from damnation, but deliverance from the consequences of sin in a believer's life. After a painful visit to the church in Corinth, Paul wrote the believers a stern letter, referred to in 2 Corinthians 2:4 but now lost to us. Although he at first regretted writing a severe reprimand to them, he later felt differently. His rebuke brought about repentance and a change of behavior. The main point is that Paul was addressing Christians, not unbelievers.

The issue is not our emotional response to our sin and guilt. What is important is knowing that we are sinners, regardless of our emotional response to that fact. In Mark 2 Jesus had a meal with people indentified as "tax collectors and sinners." The "tax collectors" were collaborators with the hated Roman government, and the "sinners" were those who in one way or another failed to observe the Jewish law. The scribes, who were experts in the Old Testament law, and the Pharisees, who were zealous adherents to the Law, were indignant. "How is it that He eats and drinks with tax collectors and sinners?" (v. 16).

Jesus replied, "Those who are well have no need of a physician, but those who are sick. I did not come to call the righteous, but sinners, to repentance" (v. 17). The scribes and Pharisees would not recognize that they were sinners as well. They saw themselves as "the righteous" who had no need of a spiritual physician. Jesus' reply was a masterful put-down of their hypocrisy and religious pretensions. His mission was to those who were spiritually sick and in need of salvation. That's why He ate dinner with those that the self-righteous scribes and Pharisees despised. The one group knew that they were sinners. The other refused to recognize their need.

Recognizing that one is a sinner is the first step in repentance. Jesus did not say that He came to make sinners feel remorse. He came to bring about repentance, a change of mind. Often it is only after we come to Christ and discover more about His righteousness and our unrighteousness that we develop a sorrow for our sin. If we do not feel worse about our sin after we come to know Christ than when we first came to Christ, it is doubtful that we have grown in our faith and walk with Christ.

KEY POINTS

Since repentance is essential to salvation, it is important to understand how it is used biblically in a salvation context.

- It implies faith or is associated with faith
- It means to change your mind, not change your life
- It is never conditioned on emotional response such as the shedding of tears

When an unbeliever comes to God as a sinner, recognizes that Christ died for his or her sins and arose from the dead, and that person trusts in Christ alone to save, both repentance and faith have taken place.

Part 5

Share What You Know

Chapter Twelve

How Do You Turn a Conversation to Spiritual Issues?

Remember when you were first trying to master the bicycle? You probably wondered if you would ever "get it." You watched others and it seemed rather easy. When you tried it, it wasn't as easy as it looked. The bruised hands, banged up knees, and injured ego were your proof. Then, all of a sudden, it came together. You probably thought, "Why was I making this so hard? It's not as tough as I thought it was."

That's similar to turning a conversation toward spiritual issues. It's not always easy. Even if others make it look like it is. At the same time, it's not as difficult as you may be making it.

What made the difference in learning to ride a bicycle is what makes the difference in learning how to turn a conversation to spiritual topics. Experience. The more experience you get, the more skilled you become at it. That is why we often explain in our training that you don't learn to evangelize after you've learned how to turn a conversation to spiritual issues. Rather, you learn how to turn a conversation to spiritual topics by evangelizing. One person at a time, one day at a time, person after person, day in and day out. That's what you take away from every encounter—experience. As one experience builds on another, you learn how to take a conversation with anyone, anywhere, and turn it to spiritual things. Those who do it well do so because they do it all the time.

In the workplace, you have a network of people who can provide those experiences. They are the people you work alongside of every day, friends and relatives of those people as well as your own friends and relatives, clients and their network of people, those through whom you receive additional training, those in your carpool, personnel in businesses from whom your company purchases supplies, parking lot employees, temporary help, and those to whom you outsource aspects of your business. The list goes on and on.

There's one principle that's needed to govern the whole process. Properly utilized, it will prevent your mind from locking up. It will also prevent you from simply memorizing key words, phrases, or questions by which you might turn a conversation. Those will hinder, not help.

I refer to this principle as "plow and pursue." Plow into the conversation and enjoy it. Relish the chance to talk. Actively engage the person in chatting. No, not talking about spiritual things, just plain talking. Have fun doing what is fun—talking to people.

As you do, pursue. Pursue any way possible to bring up spiritual topics. Note I said "any way possible." There's no set way. There are many ways to approach people with whom we are speaking. Five people may present five ways, ten people may present ten ways, and one hundred people may present one hundred ways.

The mistake often made in evangelism is memorizing a few sentences or questions we feel are "fault proof" in turning a conversation to spiritual things. Understand that these questions are often helpful and beneficial, and I have recommended some myself. Such questions may be, "Do you think people today are more confused than they used to be? What do you think the future holds for most of us?" As the conversation progresses and lends itself to a spiritual discussion, we can then ask, "Do you attend any church in the area? Have you thought much about spiritual things? In your opinion, who was Jesus Christ?"

It's one thing to be helped by those questions. It's another thing to be dependent on them. When you give yourself the freedom to think by plowing and pursuing, you realize how vast the possibilities are in transitioning to spiritual interests.

A man struggling with his marriage may give you a chance to transition into what has made your marriage work and how you found it possible to forgive one another. A person's fear of terrorist attacks might allow you to talk about how other people attempt to overcome their fears and what has helped most in your life. And *what* helped you is really *Who* helped you—Jesus Christ. A mother's struggle with her son's waywardness might allow you to introduce Someone whose shoulders can help with that load. A fellow employee's dissatisfaction with his job and a simple offer to pray for him might reveal a bit more interest in the Lord than you would have ever thought was there. Regardless of whom you meet, plow and pursue. Plowing and pursuing has been the thing that has helped me most in deciding what to say. With that "plow and pursue" principle in mind, let me lay out the process by which it works.

Talk about three areas.

There are three areas in which all non-Christians are experts regardless of whether you talk to them on the job or off the job. Those three areas are family, job, and background. In all three areas, they'll know more than you do. Additionally, the more you question them in those three areas, the more you convince them that you're interested in them as individuals. Since everyone you speak to has something different to share in those three areas, imagine how many possibilities there are to transition to spiritual topics. People are complex beings in many ways. Family, job, and background overlap in all kinds of ways. Through an engineering job, a man may have met his wife and discovered that they were both reared in the same hometown. That "coincidence" may allow you to mention something unusual in your own life and even cause you to remark, "I think there was a loving God behind everything that was happening to me." Watch their reaction. Sooner than you think, you may be discussing spiritual things.

Now you know why those who are good listeners are the best at turning conversations into spiritual discussions. Note I said "good listeners," not good talkers. Yes you do need to talk, but more importantly, you need to get them talking while you listen. The more they talk, the more you open up possibilities for you to introduce a spiritual note into the conversation.

Now let's go back to an earlier point—we learn by doing. We also now know why those who evangelize often are the best at transitioning to spiritual issues. Those who do it well do it often. The more often they do it, the more they learn how to transition to spiritual matters. A comment made to a fellow employee that started a conversation about the Lord ends up being helpful at another time. God honors obedience and uses experience. As we obey and get experience, God helps us to be more and more effective in turning conversation to the gospel. Don't be a person who presents Christ once a year. Be a person who shares the gospel at every opportunity. Keep evangelizing and keep learning.

Go from the secular to the spiritual.

As you transition, you're not attempting to go from the secular to the gospel. That seldom works. It's far too abrupt. To talk about family, job, and background and then say, "Well let me ask you something. Do you know if you'll go to heaven when you die?" Or "Let me change the subject. Have you come to a point in your life where you feel you have a relationship with God?" The other person has every reason to think, "How did we get on that subject?"

It's the spiritual subject that will allow you to later transition to sharing the gospel. Those spiritual subjects are as numerous as the ways of transitioning to spiritual things. They include prayer, religion, prophesy, church, miracles, creeds, the Bible, preachers, religious books, angels, the supernatural, the Ten Commandments, religious gatherings, Easter, Christmas, baptism, communion, spiritual principles related to happiness, the meaning of life, or money management. Keep in mind I'm using the word *spiritual* in its broadest possible sense.

Here are some examples of how these transitions can take place.

A person mentions that something very difficult happened in his home life. A simple response such as, "I'm sorry to hear that.

I promise to pray for you," might cause him to say, "I can sure use that."

Reflecting on the past Sunday, a co-worker might mention a great restaurant he and his wife went to after church. That allows you to say, "By the way, what church do you attend?"

If a person confesses that she normally doesn't go to church but probably will since Easter is coming up, that allows you to say, "What do you enjoy most about Easter services?"

If a co-worker reflects on the past devastating earthquakes around the world, he might add, "Sometimes I wonder if this world is going to be here ten years from now." Your comment could easily be, "I've done some studying on biblical prophecy. Have you ever read anything in the area of future predictions?"

You may discover that a co-worker is having a baby. That allows you to reflect on your first child and a book you read on how to raise a child God's way.

Many marriages face financial pressure due to uncontrolled spending. That allows you to mention principles you've discovered about money management based on biblical principles.

Don't claim to identify where you can't, but as you talk about family, job, and background (and pray as you talk), there comes a way to transition into something spiritual.

What happens if you see no opening to transition? There are at least two things to keep in mind. First, as you're talking to them, talk to God. You can do both at the same time because He hears the whispers of the heart. Remember, He is even more concerned about the lost than you are. Often I've said to God, "Help me find a way to transition into spiritual things." I can't remember one time that prayer has not been answered.

Second, keep talking. The longer you talk, the more the possibilities of transitioning to spiritual issues. It's virtually impossible to have an extended conversation and not find a way to transition.

Remember, if the lost person doesn't mention something that allows you to transition easily, you can. Keep in mind the principle of "plow and pursue." You're on a search to find a way to turn the direction of the conversation. You can easily make comments such as:

- "Sunday is pretty relaxing around our house. My wife and I really enjoy our church, but when we come home, we then enjoy just having family time together."
- "Financial struggles are hard. I had a difficult time in that area myself some time ago. I honestly think I prayed the hardest I've ever prayed in all my life. It's times like that I wish I prayed more all the time."
- "Like you, I like to read. Lately, I've done lots of reading about prophecy and future events. Some things I've found in that area are very interesting."

Remember the importance of listening! You may find a response that allows you to transition to spiritual matters. Until it does—plow and pursue.

Go from the spiritual to the gospel.

You have a very specific message you want to share with the lost. It's contained in ten words. "Christ died for our sins and rose from the dead." If you have now transitioned to spiritual issues, your next question can be very specific. It takes several forms but gets to the same end. Here are some examples of questions that can be used:

- "Has anyone ever taken a Bible and shown you how you can know for sure you're going to heaven?"
- "Do you feel you've ever come to know God personally or are you somewhere along the way? How far along are you?"
- "What do you think you have to do to live forever? Has anyone shown you what the Bible says?"
- "Has anyone ever shown you in the Bible how you can have a relationship with God that never ends?"

The conversation (or conversations) you've had up to this point has built a relationship that now allows you to be very direct and specific. The spiritual subjects thus far had been broad and general.

The gospel, though, is a very specific message about a very specific need—the need for an eternal relationship with God.

Present the gospel.

It's now that you explain the gospel. Remember three basic truths that make up the gospel message: (1) We are sinners, (2) Christ died for us and rose from the dead, and (3) we have to trust in Christ alone as our only way to heaven. Remember, be clear, be clear, and be clear. Salvation is received by trusting Christ alone as one's only way to heaven. Not Christ-plus-something-else, but Christ—period.

Once you've explained the gospel, it's now most appropriate to say, "Would you like to pray right now and tell God you're trusting Christ and you're on your way to heaven?" You might say, "I can pray aloud, and you can pray after me." Often, that is what they prefer. I always remind them that saying a prayer doesn't save, but it's trusting Christ that saves. The prayer at the end of the "Bad News/Good News" approach explained in chapter 13 is an example of the prayer you can use.

KEY POINTS

Turning a conversation to spiritual subjects is not always easy, but it's not as difficult as we often make it. Learn to:

- "Plow and pursue."
- Talk about their family, job, and background.
- Go from something secular to something spiritual.
- Go from the spiritual to the gospel.
- Present the gospel.

The more you do it, the better you become at it.

Chapter Thirteen

What Is an Effective Method for Explaining the Gospel?

The question posed by this chapter is a good one, but sometimes there is a concern behind the question. Someone might wonder, "If you have a particular method to share the gospel, doesn't that come across as a canned approach?" By "canned" they probably mean mechanical, memorized, insensitive, and purely by memory— without much thought or feeling. The truth is that more often than not, we'd have to admit our methods are often just that.

An effective method for explaining the gospel is just the opposite. When a method comes across as canned, it's more likely because of the presenter, not the presentation. Having a particular method of sharing the gospel allows you to be warm, sensitive, caring, and attentive. Knowing how you're going to present the gospel allows you to relax, watch the person's eyes and facial expressions, listen to every word he or she says, and even listen to how the words are said. Why? Again, because you're relaxed. You know exactly how you're going to present the gospel and even have the confidence you can do it. That's why once you have a method, it increases your confidence and your consistency in evangelism. In fact, I've never met anyone who is consistent in evangelism that does not have a basic method he or she uses.

In class at Dallas Theological Seminary, I addressed the fact that having a method helps, not hinders our efforts in evangelism.

After class, I interacted with one of the students about the importance of having a method. A few days later, I received this e-mail:

> Thanks for your time yesterday after our evangelism class at DTS. My experience with my son is such a blessing, I had to share the news with you.
>
> As I stated, I was an initial skeptic of your gospel presentation because I was considering it "canned" and thus not personal or "relational." However, the more I listened to your message and was impacted by your sincerity, the more open I became to using your method. The Lord was really working on me and my fear and complacency when it came to sharing the gospel with the people I love.
>
> My son is 32 years old and has been running from God since he was 16. Although he seemed to have an encounter with the Lord when he was 10, his spiritual rebellion had me obviously doubting his salvation. He had been searching over the last two years and had starting reading the Bible on his own. Thus, I had been praying for an opportunity to have a serious faith discussion. I was fearful of such a discussion because he had avoided these discussions in the past.
>
> I committed to using your presentation, prayed, and was surprised by the feeling of confidence I was having going into my conversation with my son. After talking for some time, sharing my personal testimony, and sharing the gospel according to your outline, I asked Jud, "Have you ever come to the point in all your spiritual journeys where you have trusted Christ as your Savior?" Larry, he looked me directly in the eyes and said, "Dad, yes I have. I had a real faith experience when I was 10, and my belief has been confirmed over the last year." I then asked him if he knew for sure that he would spend eternity with God. He again answered firmly with a "yes."
>
> I wanted you to know this because it is a real example of how your outline of the gospel gave me the confidence to present the gospel and then ask the questions that would confirm exactly where a person is in his faith. I have moved

from being a fearful skeptic of using such an outline to an excited and more prepared believer who really wants to share the gospel with those I love.

Years ago I spoke in Lubbock, Texas. A woman came up to me and said, "I mastered your method of presenting the gospel, the Bad News/Good News approach. Yesterday, I talked to my first person about the Lord, and I'm so excited about evangelism."

Notice that I consistently use the phrase "master a method," not "memorize a method." Yes, the method is memorized. There is nothing wrong in being able to quote it word for word if you're asked to, but more importantly, it's mastered. You have so mastered the method that it has mastered you. That means it gives you freedom to go into it differently or come out of it differently. You may vary an illustration, expand a particular point, or add an additional thought. That's why the approach, used properly, doesn't come across as memorized. It's simply you at your best in evangelism.

It's also important that the method be one that's easy to master and easy to follow. Otherwise, it will be confusing to non-Christians. That in itself is a problem. The gospel is a very clear and simple message—Christ died for our sins and rose from the dead. Why confuse some with the message by using a confusing method of presenting it? Think of talking with a lost person and having to say, "Now, let's see, what is point 2 and sub point b?" You end up feeling defeated and discouraged.

Here's a method I've used for years. In a nutshell, I came to Christ through God taking me from the creation (a love for the outdoors) to the Creator to Christ. It was through my own Bible study that I came to trust Christ. Immediately I thought, "I want to tell someone." I began with my liberal denominational pastor. Unfortunately, he was not my first convert! By having a passion for simplicity and clarity as I grew in the Lord and grew physically, I developed the Bad News/Good News approach. Since then, we've taught it to millions. Nothing we have done has received a greater response. People often lead their first person to Christ using this method. (The booklet form of this method can be found in the appendix to this book.)

The Bad News/Good News Method

I have little patience with evangelists who lambaste and berate believers because they don't evangelize. The reason is simple: it took me only a few years in evangelism to discover that most people would like to lead at least one person to Christ before they die. Their problem is they just don't know how.

Anyone consistent in evangelism has a basic method of speaking to others about the Lord. I honestly don't know how many have told me that the most helpful thing I ever did for them was to teach the Bad News/Good News approach.

When speaking with an unbeliever, I begin by asking questions to get to know the individual. My questions, as suggested earlier, usually concern the person's background, family, and job. As we talk, I turn the conversation to spiritual things.

Then, in preparation for presenting the gospel, I ask a question which focuses on salvation: "Has anyone ever taken a Bible and shown you how you can know you're going to heaven?" The usual reply is, "No, I don't believe anyone has." I then ask, "May I?"

At this point, I need a smooth transition into my presentation, so I say, "The Bible contains both bad news and good news. The bad news is something about you. The good news is something about God. Let's talk about the bad news first."

We are all sinners (Rom. 3:23).

I begin by saying, "There are several things you need to understand. The first is that we are all sinners." I turn to Romans 3:23 and have the person read it. The verse says, "For all have sinned and fall short of the glory of God."

Using an illustration to explain that verse, I say, "When the Bible says you and I have sinned, it means we lie, lust, hate, steal, murder, etc. The word *sin* in the Bible actually means 'to miss the mark.' In other words, God is perfect and we aren't. Let me explain. Suppose you and I were each to pick up a rock. Then I said to you, 'I want you to throw that rock and hit the North Pole.' Well, you might throw it farther than I can, or I might throw it farther than you can, but neither of us would make it. Both of us would fall short. When the Bible says that all have sinned and fall short of the glory of God, it means God has set a standard that every one of us must meet. That standard is God Himself. We must be as holy as He is holy, as perfect as He is perfect. But it doesn't matter how religiously we live or how good we are, we cannot meet the standard. All of us have sinned and fall short of the glory of God."

The penalty for sin is death (Rom. 6:23).

I introduce the second point of my outline by saying, "But the bad news gets worse. The second thing you need to understand is that the penalty for sin is death." I turn to Romans 6:23 and have the person read to the comma. Even non-Christians who have never picked up a Bible know how to stop at a comma. It says, "For the wages of sin is death."

Again I use an illustration: "Suppose you were to work for me for one day and I were to pay you fifty dollars. Fifty dollars would be your wages. It represents what you have earned. The Bible says that because you and I have sinned, we have earned death. We are going to die and be eternally separated from God."

Having presented the bad news, I now need a transition into the good news, which begins the third point of my outline. So I say, "Now I think you'll agree with me, that is bad news." The usual reply is, "Yes, I see what you mean." Then I explain, "But after the Bible gives the bad news, it gives the good news. What the Bible says is that since there is no way you could come to God, God decided to come to you."

Christ died for you (Rom. 5:8).

I continue by saying, "The third thing you need to understand is that Christ died for you." I turn to Romans 5:8 and have the person read it. "But God demonstrates His own love toward us, in that while we were still sinners, Christ died for us."

I use this illustration to explain the verse: "Let's say you were in the hospital dying of cancer. I could come to you and say, 'I want to do something for you. We'll take the cancer cells from your body and put them into my body. What would happen to me?' The usual reply is, 'You would die.' I say, 'Right. I would die. What would happen to you?' The usual reply is, 'I would live.' I then say, 'Right. You would live. Now tell me why.' 'Because you took my cancer. You died for me.' I then explain, 'Yes! I took the thing that was causing your death, placed it upon myself, and died as your substitute. The Bible says that Christ came into the world, took the sin that was causing your death, placed it upon Himself, and died in your place. He was your substitute. The third day He arose from the dead as proof that sin and death had been conquered.'"

You can be saved through faith (Eph. 2:8–9).

I introduce the final point of my outline by saying, "Now, just as the bad news got even worse, the good news gets even better. The final thing you need to understand is that you can be saved through faith." I turn to Ephesians 2:8–9 and have the person read it. It says, "For by grace you have been saved through faith, and that not of yourselves; it is the gift of God, not of works, lest anyone should boast."

I explain, "The word *grace* means undeserved or unmerited favor. *Saved* means to be rescued or delivered from the penalty of sin. Now, you are probably wondering, 'What is faith?' The word *faith* means trust."

I again use an illustration to explain the Scripture. I say, "Since Jesus Christ has died for your sins, God can now give you heaven as a free gift. All you need to do is put your faith or your trust in Christ. For example, you were not there when that chair you are sitting in was made, and you didn't examine how it was built before you sat down. You are simply trusting the chair to hold you.

Putting your faith in Christ means trusting Him to save you—not trusting your church membership, your good life, or your baptism to get you to heaven, but trusting Christ and Him alone. Your trust has to be in the One who died for you and rose from the dead. It is then that God gives you heaven as a free gift."

At this point, I use a concluding question, which invites the person to trust Christ. I ask, "Is there anything that is keeping you from trusting Christ as your Savior right now?" Many times the reply is, "No, I just never understood it before." I then ask, "Would you like to pray and tell God that you are trusting His Son as your Savior?" The frequent reply is, "Yes, I would."

I then have the person tell me how I can go to heaven to make certain he understands. If he does, I do one of two things. I either lead him in prayer or have him pray. I let the person choose which he would rather do. Usually people like the idea of me praying aloud and then praying aloud with me. But before doing either, I make certain he understands that saying a prayer has never saved anyone. Prayer is only the means by which people tell God they are trusting Jesus Christ as their Savior. The prayer I have the person repeat after me goes something like this: "Dear God, I come to You now. I know that I am a sinner. I believe Christ died for me and rose from the dead. Right now, I trust Jesus Christ as my Savior. Thank You for the forgiveness and everlasting life I now have. In Jesus' name, amen."

After the person trusts Christ, I want him to understand that assurance of everlasting life is based on fact, not feeling. So I turn to John 5:24 and have the person read it. "Most assuredly, I say to you, he who hears My word and believes in Him who sent Me has everlasting life, and shall not come into judgment, but has passed from death into life."

Then I say to the person, "Now let's go back and look at each verb in the verse. It says, 'he who hears My word.' Did you do that?" He usually replies, "Yes." I continue: "'and believes in Him who sent Me.' Did you believe what God said and trust Christ as your Savior?" He says, "Yes, I did." I continue: "'has everlasting life' Does that mean later or right now?" He replies, "Right now." I read on:

"'and shall not come into judgment.' Does that say 'shall not or 'might not'?" He replies, "It says 'shall not'!" I point to the last verse and say, "'but has passed from death into life.' Does that say 'has passed' or 'will pass'?" He responds, "Has passed." I then conclude: "In other words, you now have everlasting life on the basis of fact, not feeling." I encourage the person to commit this verse to memory within twenty-four hours. Any time he does not feel saved or any time Satan makes him doubt if he is saved, I encourage him to go over that verse. Having trusted Christ, his assurance of salvation is based on fact, not feeling.

At this point, one of two things happens: (1) I arrange to get together with him at another time to talk about how to grow as a Christian; or, if that is not possible, (2) I share with him several things that will help him grow as a Christian. I emphasize prayer, Bible study (recommending he start with Philippians), baptism, and involvement in a Bible-believing church.

A thought of encouragement—once you have learned how to present the gospel, why not teach and train someone else? Few things are more rewarding than passing on to someone else something that could have eternal value in their lives as they introduce their acquaintances to Christ using what you have mastered and taught them.

KEY POINTS

Want to be clear, consistent, and confident in evangelism? Master a method. In turn it will master you. Learn the Bad News/Good News approach:

Has anyone ever taken a Bible and shown you how you can know for sure that you're going to heaven? May I?

BAD NEWS:
    We are all sinners—Romans 3:23 (illustration: rock)
    The penalty for sin is death—Romans 6:23 (illustration: wages)

GOOD NEWS:
> Christ died for you—Romans 5:8 (illustration: cancer)
> You can be saved through faith—Ephesians 2:8–9 (illustration: chair)

Is there anything keeping you from trusting Christ right now?

Having mastered a method, you'll want to talk to the lost about Christ more than ever before and with greater frequency.

Chapter Fourteen

How Do You Follow Up?

The son of a performance-driven dad, the only love and acceptance Bryan felt was from his peers. Little did he know how conditional their acceptance was. They loved and accepted him as long as he participated in their gang activities or drug trafficking. Five years in a state penitentiary "sobered him up." What it did not teach him was how to handle life and relationships. A live-in girlfriend, a two-year marriage that ended in divorce, and a job termination because of poor performance brought him to the end of himself. The speaker's message was appealing. He knew he needed Christ—the One who makes miracles out of messes. He trusted Christ for forgiveness and eternal life.

But what happened? He came through the front door of the church. Everyone was delighted to see him. Eventually, he walked out the back door. Nobody saw him again.

How do we help believers become disciples? How do we take a person who sincerely recognizes his sinfulness before God and need for a Savior and help him or her "grow in the grace and knowledge of our Lord and Savior Jesus Christ" (2 Peter 3:18)?

Is there a possibility the person did not trust Christ? Certainly. If the gospel was not made clear, a person may know the language, but not know the Lord. Some have responded to some kind of invitation to come to Christ, but because they did not trust Christ, nothing happened spiritually. It's difficult to live for Christ if a person doesn't actually know Him. But for many, the decision was very real. So why didn't they move past the point of conversion? In other words, how do we get those excited about Christ to be eager about growing spiritually and even become excited about church?

Two Cautions

One caution is that follow-up is not necessarily the job of the believer who led the lost person to Christ. Although we should have a concern that those who respond to the Holy Spirit's pleading through our witness are properly discipled, the ultimate responsibility is not ours. It is the responsibility of the local church. Ephesians 4:12–15 explains why God has given gifted people to the church:

> . . . for the equipping of the saints for the work of ministry, for the edifying of the body of Christ, till we all come to the unity of the faith and of the knowledge of the Son of God, to a perfect man, to the measure of the stature of the fullness of Christ; that we should no longer be children, tossed to and fro and carried about with every wind of doctrine, by the trickery of men, in the cunning craftiness of deceitful plotting, but, speaking the truth in love, may grow up in all things into Him who is the head—Christ.

It is easy to understand why follow-up is the responsibility of the local church. Should a large number come to Christ in a community or through workplace outreaches, practically speaking, one person or a few people cannot follow up on all the new converts. Time alone would make this impossible. In the apostle Paul's ministry alone, there were nearly forty people who worked with him in missions of follow-up. Furthermore, the believer that leads a lost person to Christ may not be the best to follow up. Someone with the spiritual gift of teaching or encouragement may make a better discipler.

The second thing to note is that the New Testament does not answer the question, "How do you assimilate new believers into the life and activity of the local church?" Instead, it answers the question, "How do you get close to a new believer?" If we get close to a new believer, we will most likely get him into our church. As we'll see in a moment, Paul spoke of caring for new converts the way a "nursing mother cherishes her own children" (1 Thess. 2:7) and "as a father does his own children" (v. 11). That relationship makes a new believer open to an invitation to attend your church. That is particularly significant since one of the most effective means of getting an un-churched person to attend church is a personal invitation from a friend.

New Testament Follow-Up on New Believers

There's no single passage in the New Testament to which we can turn to find a how-to manual on helping new believers grow in their faith. Rather, we see it modeled in the ministry of Paul as he both evangelized and encouraged new believers.

Prayer is critical.

The role of prayer in follow-up is often underemphasized. In Paul's mind, prayer appeared to be an essential part of follow-up. Consider two examples.

One is his prayer for the new converts of Ephesus as found in Ephesians 1:15–23. We read:

> Therefore I also, after I heard of your faith in the Lord Jesus and your love for all the saints, do not cease to give thanks for you, making mention of you in my prayers: that the God of our Lord Jesus Christ, the Father of glory, may give to you the spirit of wisdom and revelation in the knowledge of Him, the eyes of your understanding being enlightened; that you may know what is the hope of His calling, what are the riches of the glory of His inheritance in the saints, and what is the exceeding greatness of His power toward us who believe, according to the working of His mighty power which He worked in Christ when He raised Him from the dead

and seated Him at His right hand in the heavenly places, far above all principality and power and might and dominion, and every name that is named, not only in this age but also in that which is to come. And He put all things under His feet, and gave Him to be head over all things to the church, which is His body, the fullness of Him who fills all in all.

Paul understood their past state by nature and their present standing by grace. Before, they were without Christ; now, they are in Christ. Before, they were far from God; now, they are near. Before, they were strangers; now, they are sons. But the thing that moved him to prayer was the encouraging report he received of their present spiritual condition. His prayer was that they might continue to pursue the course they had begun and grow in their knowledge of Christ. He says, "That the God of our Lord Jesus Christ, the Father of glory, may give to you the spirit of wisdom and revelation in the knowledge of Him" (v. 17).

Now let's look at Paul's prayer for the new converts at Colosse, found in Colossians 1:9–14. We read:

For this reason we also, since the day we heard it, do not cease to pray for you, and to ask that you may be filled with the knowledge of His will in all wisdom and spiritual understanding; that you may walk worthy of the Lord, fully pleasing Him, being fruitful in every good work and increasing in the knowledge of God; strengthened with all might, according to His glorious power, for all patience and longsuffering with joy; giving thanks to the Father who has qualified us to be partakers of the inheritance of the saints in the light. He has delivered us from the power of darkness and conveyed us into the kingdom of the Son of His love, in whom we have redemption through His blood, the forgiveness of sins.

His prayer for the new converts at Colosse was that they would have wisdom and understanding (both spiritually given) that would allow them to comprehend God's desire for their lives. If they had that wisdom and direction, they would be less likely to accept the appeal and false teaching of the Gnostics.

In Paul's mind, prayer was a means of follow-up. He was aware that no matter how many times he revisited the new believers, how many fellow workers he sent to labor among them, or how much communication he maintained, their spiritual growth could only be accomplished through the Holy Spirit. His letters to the new converts of Ephesus and Colosse were both written while he was imprisoned in Rome. Even while imprisoned, Paul saw himself actively engaged in follow-up through prayer.

Flexibility is essential.

Paul's approach to follow-up was quite simple. Whatever had to be done to assist the new convert is what the new convert received. Flexibility was seen in an "I'll do what it takes" attitude. Paul's first letter to the Thessalonians is very instructive in telling us how he cared for new converts. His words are particularly interesting in light of the fact that he was with them at the most about three months. He got a lot accomplished in a short time. He explained, "as you know how *we exhorted, and comforted, and charged every one of you*, as a father does his own children" (1 Thess. 2:11, italics mine). There is not a sharp distinction between those three words. Basically, "exhort" includes the idea of laying a particular course of conduct before a person and urging him to pursue it. "Comfort" represents the need to cheer him on in the midst of trying circumstances. "Charge" means to bear witness, confirm, or testify. It depicts a solemnity and earnestness—and an urgency—behind the encouragement.

Paul practiced those three things with the Thessalonians. He exhorted them in 1 Thessalonians 4:1–2 when he said, "Finally then, brethren, we urge and exhort in the Lord Jesus that you should abound more and more, just as you received from us how you ought to walk and to please God; for you know what commandments we gave you through the Lord Jesus." He comforted them by sending Timothy to them. He explained, "(we) sent Timothy, our brother and minister of God, and our fellow laborer in the gospel of Christ, to establish you and encourage you concerning your faith, that no one should be shaken by these afflictions; for you yourselves know that we are appointed to this" (3:2–3). The urgency behind everything Paul tells the new converts demonstrates his "charging." He makes comments such as, "And we urge you, brethren . . ." (5:12).

Children born into the same physical family often differ. One may have a hearing ailment, while another suffers from a weak eye muscle. One is extremely outgoing, while another is shy. One loves books, the other sports. A parent's "I'll do what it takes" attitude can make a difference in their physical growth.

The same kind of attitude makes a difference in the spiritual growth of new converts. God saves human beings that are different and varied in their needs. One person comes to Christ from a background of drug addiction. Prior to conversion, he craved what he should have refused. Another comes to Christ as a religious legalist—extremely religious but trying to merit entrance into heaven. Another comes to Christ from a background of parental abuse. It was difficult to accept the love of a heavenly Father because she had never experienced the love of a human father. Need-oriented flexibility in follow-up is essential.

Parental attention is required.

In Paul's mind, when people came to Christ, they were not just God's children, they were his as well. He cared for them the way a parent cares for a child. Examine the following references and the words I've italicized:

For though you might have ten thousand instructors in Christ, *yet you do not have many fathers*; for in Christ Jesus I have begotten you through the gospel. (1 Cor. 4:15)

My little children, for whom I labor in birth again until Christ is formed in you. (Gal. 4:19)

But we were gentle among you, just *as a nursing mother cherishes her own children*. (1 Thess. 2:7)

So, affectionately longing for you, we were well pleased to impart to you not only the gospel of God, but also *our own lives, because you had become dear to us*. (1 Thess. 2:8)

As you know how we exhorted, and comforted, and charged every one of you, *as a father does his own children*. (1 Thess. 2:11)

The terms *father*, *my little children*, *nursing mother*, and *dear to us* all depict an attitude of parental attention. Even the phrase *every one of you* in 1 Thessalonians 2:11 stresses the individual approach Paul used with new converts. Dawson Trotman, founder of the evangelism organization The Navigators, wrote, "Is the answer merely materials to distribute to those who come to Christ? No, it is always from the experience of successful follow-up programs, both in the New Testament and out of it, that follow-up is done by someone, not by something."[1]

Parental attention provides a basis for effective follow-up by focusing on the needs of the new convert to whatever degree necessary. With an "I'll do what it takes" attitude, parental attention reveals how best to help a new believer.

Time and hard work are needed.

"Follow-up made easy" doesn't exist. Proper follow-up requires time and hard work.

It is worth noting that each missionary journey the apostle Paul took increased in length by at least one year because of his visits to places he had previously ministered. Paul went back to visit the people and confirm churches in at least nine of the places he evangelized.

Paul spoke of the hard work often involved. He says, "Him we preach, warning every man and teaching every man in all wisdom, that we may present every man perfect in Christ Jesus. To this end I also labor, striving according to His working which works in me mightily" (Col. 1:28–29). "Labor" depicts work that can sometimes be exhausting, work that sometimes makes one weary. "Striving" conveys the idea of agonizing. As a general rule, follow-up is more difficult than evangelism. Dawson Trotman also said, "You can lead a soul to Christ in twenty minutes to a couple of hours. But it takes from twenty weeks to a couple of years to get him on the road to maturity."[2]

The times of hard work are worth it. Paul testified, "For what is our hope, or joy, or crown of rejoicing? Is it not even you in the presence of our Lord Jesus Christ at His coming? For you are our glory and joy" (1 Thess. 2:19–20). A person who leads another to Christ or assists in his growth will rejoice when the new convert stands before the Lord.

The goal is maturity.

The first thing we often suggest to new converts is their need to find a church to attend or a Bible study to begin. However, those are the means to the end. They are not the end. The goal is maturity.

Paul says, "Him we preach, warning every man and teaching every man in all wisdom, that we may present every man perfect in Christ Jesus. To this end I also labor, striving according to His working which works in me mightily" (Col. 1:28–29). *Perfect* conveys the idea of maturity and completion. Only when a person was mature in Christ did Paul feel his labors and the labors of others had been completed.

There is an extent to which that growth to maturity is a life-long process. Although it can be said of someone, "She is a mature believer," no one can ever look back and say, "I've arrived." The most we can say is, "I'm consistently moving along on the path to greater maturity." Everything used to enhance that growth is the means, not the end.

It is important to convey the proper goal of spiritual growth to new converts. Otherwise, they may do one of two things. They may settle on an activity such as going to church without examining the "why" behind what they are doing. Second, they may settle for less than what they should in terms of the degree of spiritual maturity for which they strive

Steps to Assist a New Convert in Spiritual Growth

With the Scriptural approach to follow-up understood, how do we practically disciple a new convert?

Meet with a new believer sooner rather than later.

As soon as possible (the sooner the better), the discipler should meet with the new convert personally and privately. It is important to do three things during that time:

1. Check understanding of the gospel. It's helpful to review what you are now hopeful he or she understands. Effective questions are ones such as:

   - If you were to die right now, where would you go?
   - If you stood before God right now and He were to ask you, "Why should I let you into heaven?" what would you say?
   - Where would you go if you were to die five years from now?
   - Suppose tomorrow you explode in a fit of anger because of an unexpected criticism and died of a heart attack. Where would you go?

2. Give assurance of salvation. As I mentioned in the previous chapter, one of the best verses to use is John 5:24: "Most assuredly, I say to you, he who hears My word and believes in Him who sent Me has everlasting life, and shall not come into judgment, but has passed from death into life." Have a new believer interact with that verse by asking the following questions:

- "he who hears My word"—Did you do that?
- "and believes in Him who sent Me"—Did you believe what God said and trust Christ as your Savior?
- "has everlasting life"—Does that mean later or right now?
- "and shall not come into judgment"—Does that say "shall not" or "might not"?
- "but has passed from death into life"—Does that say "shall pass" or "has passed"?

3. Encourage a new believer to memorize that verse within the next twenty-four hours. Explain that Satan may cause doubt about salvation, and there may be days when he or she does not necessarily "feel" saved. Eternal life is based on fact, not feelings. God said it; that settles it.

Talk with a new believer about spiritual growth. Provide a follow-up booklet written on a new believer's level that is biblically based. Many have been helped by EvanTell's two books *Welcome to the Family* (a Bible study) and *31 Days to Living as a New Believer* (a devotional).

Meet with a new believer one-on-one for eight weeks.

Assure a new believer that growth doesn't happen overnight. It takes time and effort. Ask him or her to meet with you once a week for eight weeks to get started. This kind of challenge can sometimes be threatening to a new believer. If it is, ask him or her to take it one week at a time. Each week look at the possibility of meeting again the next week. Patience and sensitivity are essential with anyone, but particularly with new believers.

Group meetings with new converts can be helpful, but don't neglect individual attention. Although the circumstances and problems of new converts may be similar, no two are alike. Meeting with new believers one-on-one allows for personal attention to their situations and provides a basis for the required flexibility.

Who should serve as disciplers? To avoid temptation and even the appearance of evil (1 Thess. 5:22), disciplers should work with a believer of the same gender. The discipler should also be a growing believer. Spiritually, the issue is not *where* we are now, but *the direction* in which we are headed. A stagnant believer is going to find it difficult to help a new convert. The new convert may also be hindered instead of helped by a fellow believer who is spiritually at a standstill. It is important to place the right believer as a discipler for a new convert.

A discipler also needs to be a patient person—one who does not get easily frustrated. New converts proceed at varying speeds of growth. Some believers expect a new convert to be in one month at a point they themselves did not achieve for two years. Patience is critical.

The discipler should also be willing to commit time. Meeting with the new convert once a week for eight weeks is time-consuming. The discipler cannot say, "I think I can do that." He must say, "I will do that."

What do you cover during that eight-week series? The follow-up material provided at your first visit should assist in covering at least five subjects:

Salvation. First, review the gospel of Jesus Christ and what it means to believe (trust) in Christ alone for salvation. You want to firmly implant in the convert's mind and heart that salvation is not a matter of what he has done for Christ, but what Christ did for him on a cross. Although you reviewed this on your initial visit, you want to review it again so he is certain to understand the freeness and certainty of his salvation. Be sensitive to the fact that some may have only thought they understood the gospel when they responded to your invitation. They may come to grips with the freeness of salvation and actually trust Christ in the process of follow-up.

Spiritual growth through Bible study and prayer. Remind the convert that spiritual growth comes through communication. God desires to talk to him through the Bible. He needs to talk to God through prayer. Encourage him to start with the book of Philippians and read one chapter each day, staying in that book for a month. The repeated reading of passages allows him to learn truths he may have missed earlier. Ask him to concentrate on one thing he's learned each day that he can meditate on throughout the day. Philippians is the best book to begin with because it talks about daily Christian living and is the easiest book of the entire Bible for a new Christian to understand.

Baptism. Explain that in the New Testament, those who believed were baptized. A helpful verse is Acts 2:41, which reads, "Then those who gladly received his word were baptized." It is important to stress that baptism has no saving value. It is the first step of discipleship and the way to publicly tell others, "I belong to Christ and desire to follow Him." Assist the convert in arranging a time when he can be baptized.

Fellowship with other believers. Explain that church attendance is important because of our need to be encouraged by other believers who also desire to grow spiritually. Hebrews 10:24–25 says, "And let us consider one another in order to stir up love and good works, not forsaking the assembling of ourselves together." Believers need one another; we go to church to give, not merely to get. Even if one's knowledge of the Word is limited, he can pray with other believers, study with them, and encourage them.

It's best to take the new convert with you to church. New believers often feel awkward walking into a crowd of people they've never been with before. If that is not possible, ask another believer to take the new believer along and introduce him to others. If there is no way you can take him or even find someone else to do so, explain what a Bible-teaching church is and encourage him to find one. Explain that a Bible-teaching church is one where each Sunday the pastor takes a different passage of the Bible and explains it.

Evangelism. Teach the basic elements of the gospel: Christ died for our sins and rose from the dead. Teach the new convert a method you've found effective for sharing the gospel with others. Every person consistent in evangelism uses a basic method. Take him with you and let him observe you evangelizing non-Christians. Evangelism cannot be mastered apart from actually speaking with unbelievers.

Organize a band of people who will pray for new converts.

As seen in Paul's ministry, prayer is an important part of follow-up. Organize a group of people who will pray by name for new converts. This is a great way to involve senior believers or those in the church who have limited mobility due to physical limitations or illness. They are often mature believers who are deeply committed to prayer and have time to commit to prayer. First Timothy 5:5 speaks of the ministry widows have in prayer: "Now she who is really a widow, and left alone, trusts in God and continues in supplications and prayers night and day." These are believers for whom prayer is not an "off and on" activity, but something they continue in day and night. The ministry they can have in praying for new converts can be tremendously effective.

As they pray, they need to pray for specific needs. Notice again the specific requests Paul made to God on behalf of the Colossians: "For this reason we also, since the day we heard it, do not cease to pray for you, and to ask that you may be filled with the knowledge of His will in all wisdom and spiritual understanding" (Col. 1:9). His specific request was that they might have wisdom and understanding of all things spiritual. Why? He continues, "That you may walk worthy of the Lord, fully pleasing Him, being fruitful in every good work and increasing in the knowledge of God; strengthened with all might, according to His glorious power, for all patience and longsuffering with joy" (vv. 10–11). A person who has wisdom and understanding of all things spiritual tries to please the Lord in all things, bears fruit in all kinds of good deeds, and responds properly to difficult situations and people. Five specific areas where they should talk to God on behalf of new converts are:

- That they will grow in their knowledge of Him
- That God will help them adjust to their new life
- That they will have wisdom and understanding in how to live for Christ
- That God will help them take out of their lives what shouldn't be there and put in what should be there
- That God will use them to reach unbelieving friends, family, and acquaintances

You don't need a lot of people praying. A few praying fervently and expectantly will make the difference.

Involve new converts.

As you disciple and pray for new believers, don't forget to involve them. Seek out "handle-able" tasks that assist in furthering the work of God's kingdom. It may involve a building or cleaning project around the church, participation in a community outreach event, or preparation of materials for a Sunday school class or small group meeting. One church I know of used the skill and talent of a new convert in renovating a picnic area on the church lawn that was often used for church gatherings. The point is to help them feel a part of what's happening, whether it's something of a physical or spiritual nature.

Consider each new believer's strengths, abilities, and skills. A new convert who is a carpenter may be honored when you ask for his advice and help on a building project the church has undertaken to assist a community struck by disaster. He realizes at this early stage in his Christian growth that there is a place he can contribute. You might give new converts with acting abilities parts in a drama outreach to non-Christians. A new convert with ability in decorating might be encouraged when you ask for her assistance in decorating tables for a friendship dinner. She begins to see how her talent can be used to touch others. The ways new converts can be used are endless.

One caution—the new convert needs to be a helper, not a

leader. When Paul spoke to Timothy about the qualifications for leaders, he gave a warning about new converts. He explains, "not a novice, lest being puffed up with pride he fall into the same condemnation as the devil" (1 Tim. 3:6). Choosing a new convert to be a leader can have disastrous results for him or her. Rapid advancement to leadership without time for spiritual growth can fill a new believer with an inflated ego or self-conceit, the same sin that caused Satan's downfall (Ezek. 28:11–19).

KEY POINTS

Where does the responsibility for follow-up lie? The new convert must show a desire to grow. We cannot do for new believers what they have no interest in doing for themselves. Responsibility for follow-up, however, also rests upon the believer doing the discipling. Follow-up is done by some*one*, not some*thing*. That someone needs to understand that:

- Prayer is critical
- Flexibility is essential
- Parental attention is required
- Time and hard work are needed
- The goal is maturity

When we follow the New Testament model for follow-up, there will be many new converts characterized by Paul's words to the Thessalonians: "For what is our hope, or joy, or crown of rejoicing? Is it not even you in the presence of our Lord Jesus Christ at His coming? For you are our glory and joy" (1 Thess. 2:19–20).

Part 6

Use Public Speaking Opportunities

Chapter Fifteen

Can Anyone Learn Public Speaking in the Workplace?

It's been true for years and still is—ask anyone, "What are your two biggest fears?" More often than not, they will quickly answer, "Flying in an airplane and speaking in public." Some feel those two events have one thing in common. They both can lead to a crash landing!

Public speaking isn't for everyone. God gifts and equips people differently, and if public speaking is not your "thing," there is no need to apologize. But the old axiom has some bearing here— "Don't knock it till you've tried it."

Why? Because some people have more ability in public speaking than they've ever admitted or known because they've never tried it. They have just assumed they can't do it. Don't limit your potential by unproven assumptions! There may be untapped abilities that have simply been pushed into the corner by lack of experience. How many times have you met people who refer to something they now do and delight in doing? Then they remarked, "But I never thought I'd be doing this!"

I'm one of those people. I love to water ski. Gliding across the water gives me a high that is taller than the trees embracing the shoreline. If you had told me fifty years ago that one day I'd be an avid skier, I would have retorted, "You must have another Larry

Moyer in mind, or else you're losing your mind!" Prior to coming to Christ, my fear of water was greater than the fear of hell. Sincerely! I have no idea why, but the fear was real. A few trusted friends made the difference. First, they convinced me that with my love of the outdoors and physically demanding sports, I would love it. Then they showed me and convinced me that life jackets really do hold a person up, something of which I was not convinced. The rest is history. If someone says, "Let's go waterskiing," I only have two questions—where and how soon? Had I not tried it, I would never have known how much I enjoy it. The point? Give yourself a chance. If you decide it's not for you, you will know why. But how will you know until you try it? There are several reasons I urge you to try.

Speaking is communication.

One, speaking is, first and foremost, communication. If a person is effective in communicating an idea one-to-one in the workplace, there is a good chance he or she can communicate an idea one-to-fifty, or one-to-one hundred. The biggest difference simply is the number of people on the other side.

The past can't control the present.

Sometimes people toss aside the idea of public speaking because of one poor experience in the past. "Well, one time I tried it and . . . ." Remember: life changes and so do people. A variety of factors may have made for that one bad experience, a majority of which may have had nothing to do with you. Forgetting can be a blessing when it allows you to move on to something that deserves a second chance. Why let the past intimidate you when the future awaits you?

It's a stewardship issue.

Think of the fact that you are the manager of everything you have, not the owner. That includes your tongue, lips, and voice—

everything. You manage them, but God owns them. If indeed public speaking is something you could be better at than you give yourself credit for, why wouldn't you want to use this gift in the most effective way possible? Speaking to someone one-to-one is always essential, but if you have something important to say and you can say it to fifty or one hundred instead of one, you increase your impact.

It gets you outside your comfort zone.

The fear of public speaking is often not as paralyzing as you think it is. It may just be a matter of being pushed out of your comfort zone and doing something you've never done. You know how to run a department at your office, negotiate a deal with a tough client, participate in labor negotiations, or organize a community pledge drive. You've faced challenges and risen to the occasion. Sure, these situations may have been out of your comfort zone, and they felt difficult for you at first. Once you moved forward, however, you most likely found the going got easier. A little push from someone like me may be just what you need to introduce you to an opportunity you may wish you had taken advantage of sooner.

It's not going to be your vocation.

Finally, you may not want to spend your life doing public speaking, but that doesn't mean you couldn't do it once or twice a year. A friend of mine does not see himself as a public speaker and doesn't aspire to be one. But I've heard him comment on several occasions, "It's something I can do if I need to. It's not something I relish." There's absolutely nothing wrong with those sentiments. But doing it on occasion allows God to use him in that capacity if He so desires. Don't fall into thinking that to do it occasionally means you have to do it all the time.

KEY POINTS

Public speaking is not for everyone. But it is for many, and it may be for you. What do you have to lose by opening the door? After all, consider this:

- Speaking is communication—something you do daily.
- The past can't control the present.
- It's a stewardship issue.
- It gets you outside your comfort zone.
- It's not going to be your vocation.

You may find yourself saying, "Thanks, Lord! With your help, I am better at this than I thought I was."

Chapter Sixteen

What's Important in Speaking in the Workplace?

One of the most quoted lines from the "Peanuts" cartoon strip by late Charles M. Schultz are the words of Linus: "There is no greater burden than great potential."

That is the burden every believer in the workplace ought to feel—the burden of the enormous potential in being an evangelistic speaker in the workplace. There are far too few of them. Speakers in the workplace abound, but evangelistic speakers in the workplace are too few.

It is important, however, to put first things first. We need to examine how and where workplace leaders learn to speak as well as the type of evangelistic messages they can give. Let's first examine what is important in speaking as a workplace leader.

Always make the gospel clear.

There are mistakes that can be made as a speaker in the workplace. The one mistake that ought never be made is to make the gospel unclear. You are dealing with eternal issues. A person's eternal destiny is being addressed. As you present the gospel in the workplace, three things must be stressed.

The first is that we are sinners. We have rebelled against God and missed His standard of perfection. God's standard is not the preacher at our church, our neighbor, or best friend; it is Christ Himself. Alongside of Him, we have all come short and missed His standard. God, being a holy and righteous God, has no choice but to punish sin. Hence, all people face eternal separation from God in what the Bible calls hell.

Second, our audience must understand that Christ died for us and rose again. Note the words "for us." He did not die to show us how to live or for that matter show us how to die by putting others first. He died as our substitute. Had He not died, we would have. He took the punishment for our sins, died in our place, and rose the third day. His resurrection the third day proved that He was the perfect Son of God and God had accepted His sin payment for our sin problem.

Third, we must explain that the way we receive His pardon and gift of eternal life is through believing—trusting—Christ alone as our only way to heaven. We are speaking to a workplace audience accustomed to earning everything they have, from their clothing, paychecks, and benefits to their bonuses, retirement programs, and stock options. Therefore, it must be stressed that eternal life is a gift—completely free. It cannot be earned or merited. We must also stress that it is Christ alone that saves, not Christ-plus-anything we are or have done

Keep in mind that many of those in the workplace take pride in their earning accomplishments, so the idea of accepting a gift may be more difficult for them to grasp. That is why the gospel must be made clear. They must understand that unless they receive eternal life as a completely free gift, they cannot have it.

As mentioned previously, whether we present the message of salvation in a few minutes or half an hour, we dare not speak confusingly where God speaks clearly. Always make the gospel clear.

Recognize your advantages.

Don't think that as a workplace speaker you are at a disadvantage because you may have never been to Bible college or seminary.

The fact is, you have the advantage of knowing and being known by the people you are addressing.

Evangelistic speaking doesn't begin in the study, it begins on the sidewalk. There are three things you must know about non-Christians to speak effectively to them. You must know how they think, how they talk, and what they talk about. Church leaders who are not around non-Christians have to make a special effort as they speak evangelistically to remind themselves of where non-Christians are. You already know. You do business with them, work alongside of them, and interact with them over lunch. You observe everything: the mood with which they come to work, the words they let "slip" in their conversations, the things that depress them about life and people, what they enjoy and don't enjoy about work, and even comments they make about life after death. You may have things to learn about speaking, but be encouraged—you already know your audience.

Another advantage you have is that you have already developed your skills in communication. In the workplace, you've not only learned how unbelievers think, but also how to get people to think. Otherwise, you couldn't get your ideas across. Having learned communication skills in the workplace, you are now taking those skills and putting them into practice in evangelistic speaking.

Wrap your speech around a single idea.

Usually, the most that the average person can remember at one sitting is one thing. That is why the more you wrap your entire message around a single purposefully communicated idea, the better. (I will show you how to do that with a sample message in chapter 21.)

By asking, "What am I talking about?" and then, "What am I saying about that subject?" you can reduce your message to one sentence. The danger in speaking is not trying to say too little—it's trying to say too much. Once you've decided upon the one idea you want to communicate to your audience, you can then ask, "What needs to be put into my speech and what can be left out?"

You can't—and should not—try to say everything. You want to say what's most important in communicating your main idea. It is far more preferable that your audience leaves with one idea they can never forget instead of many ideas they will never remember. Wrapping your message around a single idea helps make you a communicator instead of just a speaker in the workplace. That is why God has you there—to communicate, not just to speak.

Don't talk too long.

Not only do speakers of all kinds try to say too much, our other mistake is that we talk too long.

Don't take ten minutes to say what could be said in five. Don't take twenty minutes to say what could be said in fifteen. Here again is where wrapping everything you say around a central idea will help. It will enable you to keep your message shorter as you examine not what could be said, but what needs to be said.

I've never seen an audience upset because a speaker stopped before they thought he would. I have seen many audiences who get upset because a speaker went longer than necessary. Brevity is always a plus, never a minus. A person once said that he was taught three things in speaking: be sincere, be brief, be seated. Don't focus on filling your "time slot." Focus on saying what you need to say as succinctly as possible. There is nothing wrong with taking twenty minutes, if that is what you were allotted, as long as it takes twenty minutes to effectively say it. There is everything wrong with speaking twenty minutes just because you were given twenty minutes.

Speak—don't preach.

In the workplace, you are not trying to do what your pastor does on a Sunday morning—preach a sermon. You are trying to do on a public level what you would do on a personal level—communicate a message. That is why the brevity of your presentation, the ease with which the audience can listen to you, and the more listeners see you as on their team, not on their back, is critical. Hopefully, this is something you already understand. I give this caution, however, because I have seen people in the workplace stand before an audience and try to be someone other than who they are or need to be. They may imitate a preacher they've observed or someone speaking to a large audience, but it made them less effective. Concentrate on speaking, not preaching.

Remember—speaking in the workplace is speaking.

Evangelistic speaking in the workplace is different than other forms of speaking, but that doesn't change the fact that evangelistic speaking is still speaking. What is important for speaking in general becomes important for evangelistic speaking in particular. Use illustrations, humor, and repetition. Combine grace and truth, and be direct without being insulting. Equally important is undergirding everything you say in prayer. You must know how to speak to God about people as you prepare to speak to people about God.

The differences in evangelistic speaking relate more to your audience, the length of time you have, and the kinds of messages you give. Approach workplace speaking knowing how it compares to speaking anywhere. The more you learn the skills involved in speaking in general, the more it will help you in evangelistic speaking.

Practice, practice, practice!

Evangelistic speakers in the workplace often don't make their living being speakers. It is not in their job descriptions. Addressing an audience through an evangelistic message is the exception, not the norm. That's why practice becomes essential.

Write your message out. Then take your manuscript and read it over and over and over. Then practice without your manuscript. Practice the way it works for you. Some like to rehearse in front of a mirror. That has never worked for me. Seeing myself in the mirror is a frightening sight! Sincerely, that is more difficult for me, not easier. Walking around in my study verbalizing what I want to say works better. Others like to get one or two friends together and practice on them. Do what works for you. But practice your message days, and preferably weeks, ahead. That practice plays a huge part in your comfort level as you stand before your audience to do the real thing. Having your message firmly in your mind through practice helps you communicate effectively to your audience when the time and pressure arrive.

KEY POINTS

Potential opportunities for speaking in the workplace abound. However, it is important that you know where to begin in taking advantage of that potential. Develop and master your potential by:

- Always making the gospel clear
- Recognizing the advantage you have by being around non-Christians
- Wrapping your speech around a single idea
- Not talking too long
- Speaking in a conversational tone instead of a preaching tone
- Knowing how evangelistic speaking compares to speaking anywhere
- Practice, practice, practice!

As you build on what you've learned speech by speech, master your skills, and take advantage of varying opportunities, you'll become an experienced and effective communicator.

Chapter Seventeen

How to Use Your Testimony as an Evangelistic Message

If you know anything about baseball, you are well aware that one of the legendary names in the games is Mickey Mantle. His statistics are amazing: 536 home runs, 1,529 RBIs, a .298 career batting average, 7 world championships, and 3 MVP awards. In 1961 alone, when he stepped up to the plate, he sent 54 balls sailing into the bleachers—just short of Babe Ruth's record. Mickey Mantle did not simply play hard in the ballpark of baseball. He played hard in the ballpark of life. One individual said about him, "He played hard and partied even harder." For him, there was no tomorrow.

Unfortunately, that led to a forty-year battle with alcohol that destroyed his body and dimmed his mind. In June 1995, doctors informed him that cancer had destroyed his liver, and Mickey realized that he was about to stare death right in the face. When Mickey was in Dallas during an All-Star break, he picked up the phone and called former Yankee second baseman Bobby Richardson, an old friend and teammate of his, as well as a committed believer. Not only did Mickey ask Bobby to pray for him, but also Mickey's family asked Bobby to come and visit him. For years, Bobby used his own testimony to speak to Mickey about his need of Jesus Christ as his personal Savior, but

Mickey never seemed to see his need. When Bobby Richardson walked into Mickey's hospital room and over to his bed, it was then that Mickey told Bobby what he had always been waiting to hear. He said, "Bobby, I've been wanting to tell you that I have trusted Jesus Christ as my Savior." You can imagine how Bobby felt. Tears came to his eyes because he knew that the one who had been a friend for life would now be a friend for eternity. In fact, some time later when Mickey was asked how he knew he would spend eternity in heaven, he quoted John 3:16: "For God so loved the world that He gave His only begotten Son, that whoever believes in Him should not perish but have everlasting life."[1]

There's no question about it. God wants to use your testimony to bring someone to faith in Jesus Christ, just as He used the testimony of Bobby Richardson in the life of Mickey Mantle. As a person in the workplace, one of the most effective messages you have is your own testimony. You may feel inadequate in explaining a particular text of Scripture as well as someone who has had special training in a Bible college or seminary. But no one can present your testimony better than you can. God wants to use what He has done in your life to explain to others what He would like to do in theirs. The advantage, too, is that this is a message that can be given in a very short period of time.

Before discussing some helpful ideas in giving an effective testimony, let's answer a basic question.

What is a testimony?

An effective testimony can best be defined by what it explains, and an effective testimony explains three things.

Where were you before you came to Christ?

One of the first things that an effective testimony does is help listeners understand what you were like before you came to Christ. It answers questions such as:

- What were your biggest struggles?
- How did you used to think?
- Did you think at all about God, Jesus Christ, and the Bible?
- Did you think about anything spiritual?
- Did you ever attend church?
- How might others have characterized you?
- Where was your life headed and how fast were you headed there?
- As well as you can remember, what were you reaching out for in life?

You don't need to answer all these questions, but the point is to help listeners understand who you were and where you were before you came to Christ. Why is that so important? As one person has said, "I'm not the person I want to be, I'm not the person I should be, but I can never be what I was." Before others can fully appreciate where you are, they need to understand where you used to be. That also communicates to unbelievers very clearly and vividly as they listen to you that if God can change your life, He can change theirs too.

How did you come to Christ?

An effective testimony does not concentrate on *when* a person came to Christ, but *how* a person came to Christ. If you remember the actual date you trusted Christ, that's fine. But emphasize how, not when. If you only emphasize when, a non-Christian will only know when you came to Christ. When you emphasize how, then they will know by listening to you how they can come to Christ as well.

Regardless of what you share about where you were when you came to Christ, you should emphasize three things: (1) you were a sinner, (2) you came to understand that Jesus Christ died in your place as your substitute and rose again, and (3) only through personal trust in Christ alone could you receive the gift of eternal life.

Notice I used the word *trust*. As mentioned earlier, stay away from phrases like "I invited Jesus into my heart," "I accepted Christ," or "I gave my life to God." The word the Bible uses is *believe*. In John 6:47 we are told, "He who believes in Me has everlasting life." To believe means to trust in Christ alone. Don't confuse your audience by using unclear terminology. Explain that you came to understand that Christ died on a cross, taking the punishment for your sin, and rose again, and only through trusting in Christ alone could you receive the gift of eternal life.

Share with your listeners how God used a friend or mate to bring you to Christ. Tell about a health problem or financial trouble that God used to get your attention. Help your listeners understand what made you start thinking about spiritual things. But regardless of who explained the gospel to you and when they explained it, first and foremost help your listeners understand what you came to understand—the good news of Christ's death and resurrection.

What difference has Christ made in your life today?

How is your life as a Christian different from what it used to be? If you were to list two or three of the most significant changes God has made in your life, what would they be? But as you list these, be certain to emphasize that you now know beyond the shadow of any doubt that if you were to die you'd go straight to heaven. That's important because, first of all, that is the emphasis of the gospel of John, the book God wrote for nonbelievers. In John 11:25–26 Jesus says, "I am the resurrection and the life. He who believes in me, though he may die, he shall live. And whoever lives and believes in Me shall never die."

A speaker once said, "God is not offering you earth with heaven thrown in. He's offering you heaven with earth thrown in." Another reason to emphasize your assurance of going to heaven is because a non-Christian may be as happy as you are, their marriages may be as healthy as yours is, but if they are honest, they have to admit that they don't know for sure that they are going to heaven. So make certain that you state clearly the most important thing that happened—you now know you are going to heaven.

Thus, an effective testimony explains these three things: (1) where you were before you came to Christ, (2) how you came to Christ, and (3) the difference Christ has made in your life today.

To see an example, look at Paul's testimony in Acts 22:3–21. It can easily be divided into three parts. Verses 3–5 explain where he was before he came to Christ. Verses 6–16 explain how he came to Christ. Then verses 17–21 explain the difference Christ has made. What worked almost two thousand years ago still works today.

Eleven Helpful Ideas

Now that you know how to structure a testimony, let me suggest some helpful ideas for giving an effective testimony.

Keep your testimony short and to the point.

Remember, this is a testimony, not a sermon. When used as an evangelistic message, a testimony ought to be kept in the range of five to seven minutes. There may be occasions when you are afforded more time, but normally you should keep it brief. Put yourself in an unbeliever's shoes. It is always better to err on the side of brevity. It has been said that some speakers are like the peace and mercy of God—they are beyond our understanding and they continue forever! You don't want your listeners to say that about your testimony! Brevity enhances communication. You strike them as someone who has something to say. You say it. Then you sit down.

Make the gospel clear.

In 1 Corinthians 15:3–5, Paul clearly stated what the gospel is: "For I delivered to you first of all that which I also received: that Christ died for our sins according to the Scriptures, and that He was buried, and that He rose again the third day according to the Scriptures, and that He was seen by Cephas, then by the twelve." Paul explained that Christ died and that He was buried. His burial was proof that He died. He arose. The proof that He arose is that He was seen. So the gospel in its simplicity is: Christ died for our sins and rose from the dead. So, as I emphasized earlier, explain to your audience that you are a sinner, you recognized that Christ died for you and rose from the dead, and you put your trust in Jesus Christ alone as your only way to heaven. Remember you are not only sharing your story. You are sharing the message of Jesus Christ. We dare not speak confusingly where God speaks clearly. Make the gospel clear.

Don't use your testimony to teach the entire Bible.

A few Scriptures properly placed and effectively used will do more than many verses. Whatever you do, don't use your testimony as a platform to demonstrate your Bible knowledge or how much of it you have memorized. Remember, this is a testimony, not a "me-i-mony." We need to impress them with our Savior, not with our knowledge of the Bible. So don't use your testimony to teach them the entire Bible. The time to teach the Bible is in follow-up, not in the giving of our testimony.

Don't talk "Christian talk."

Instead of saying, "I've been saved," explain, "I've come to a point in my life that I know beyond any shadow of a doubt that if I were to die, I'd go to heaven." If you are referring to a book in the New Testament, don't use the word *epistle*. Call it a book of the Bible, or if you're referring to a verse, say, "One of the statements in the New Testament that means a lot to me is . . ." Refer to a seat, not a pew; a song, not a hymn; an auditorium, not a sanctuary; a paragraph of the Bible, not a passage from the Bible. Don't talk Christian talk. Talk language non-Christians understand.

Be specific whenever possible.

Details are what enable your listeners to form a picture in their minds. Saying "I grew up in a religious home" is not nearly as clear as saying "I grew up in a religious home in Pennsylvania, the youngest of three children." Likewise, saying "A friend of mine told me about Christ" is not nearly as helpful as "A friend of mine I met after ten years of working at a job in an oil refinery started talking to me. I sensed that I had met someone who didn't just care about his job, but he cared about me." If you came to Christ as a teenager, it's helpful to know if you were in your early teens or late teens. Remember, you are trying to keep your testimony brief, but one sentence of details can communicate more than several sentences with no details.

Don't mention denominations.

If you grew up in a denominational church, that's all listeners really need to know. They don't need to know which denomination it was. Mentioning a denomination does more harm than good. Even though you did not mean to, it may make your listener feel that you are saying that anyone who belongs to that denomination does not know the Lord. As a non-Christian, if I am part of that denomination, that puts me on the defensive and keeps me from hearing what you have to say.

Be transparent, but don't be indiscreet.

When sharing the details of your past, there is no need to hide your drug addiction, brushes with the law, or a lack of proper standards. But we do not need to go into such detail that listeners think we are proud of what we were able to get away with. We don't want to paint the picture that ever since we have come to Christ, life has been a bed of roses. Let your listeners know that Jesus Christ saves sinners, not perfect people. At the same time, laying out certain pieces of dirty laundry could be offensive, embarrassing, and demonstrate a lack of discretion on your part.

Summarize your testimony into one sentence.

Ask yourself the question, "If I were to put my whole testimony into one sentence, what would it be?" How would you express it? I would suspect that had you asked Mickey Mantle that question, he would have said, "I'm thrilled to know Christ, but I only wish I'd done it in the first inning instead of the last." Or a man who ended up in bankruptcy and through that came to Christ might say, "I ended up at the bottom of my profession but the top of my life."

Why is a one-sentence summary important? The reason is simple. You don't want to simply instruct your listeners. You want to impact them. One sentence that tells your listeners in a nutshell what God has done in your life tends to do just that. This is a sentence you usually use toward the end of your testimony, but it ought to be a sentence that wraps up what the Lord has done. While a catchy-sounding sentence may sound impressive, it's more important to concentrate on being clear, not clever.

Think it through—Write it down—Practice giving it—Then write it again.

Let's go over those four steps again. Think it through. Write it down. Practice giving it to someone. Then write it again. By the time you have done that, you will have mastered, not memorized, your testimony, and you will be able to talk, not ramble. You will know it so well that you will know what you want to say and will be able to free up, not freeze up. That's important, because it's not only what we say, it's how we say it. Going through those four steps is worth every moment of our time and every ounce of our energy. When we share what God's done in our life in such a clear way, the non-Christian knows that He can do it in his or her life as well.

Don't hesitate to encourage interaction.

Audiences could be encouraged to interact with you in the privacy of their seats. Suppose you grew up in Chicago. It's helpful to stop and say, "Have you ever been to Chicago? Let me see your hand if you have." Not only does that bring warmth into a setting, but it also gives your testimony a conversational, not a preaching, tone. It helps your listeners know that you are talking with them, not at them. It may be helpful to share your testimony from beginning to end without interruption so listeners can see the complete picture of what the Lord did in your life. A pause, however, that encourages this kind of interaction will not deter you but help you share your testimony in a warm and personal way.

In a sample after-dinner message included in chapter 21, I refer to American Express. I explain that they advertise their services throughout the world and they do it with a very simple slogan. I then tell the audience, "If I start it, you can finish it." Then I say, "American Express . . ." I pause as the audience responds, "Don't leave home without it."

Be genuinely enthusiastic.

We will not sell them on somebody we are not sold on ourselves. They must see the happiness and sincere enthusiasm on our faces. That enthusiasm communicates to them that coming to know Jesus Christ was one of the most exciting things that has happened in our life. Your enthusiasm should communicate to unbelievers that they are missing out on Someone who is very exciting.

KEY POINTS

One of your most effective messages in the workplace is your own testimony. But that message, like any message, is only effective when it's crafted thoughtfully, biblically, and clearly. That means it should explain:

1. Where you were before you came to Christ
2. How you came to Christ
3. What difference He has made in your life today

You should be careful to:

- Keep your testimony short and to the point
- Make the gospel clear
- Not use your testimony to explain the entire Bible
- Not talk Christian talk
- Be specific whenever possible
- Not mention denominations
- Be honest, but not indiscreet
- Summarize your testimony into one sentence
- Think it through, write it down, give it to someone else, then write it again
- Encourage audience interaction
- Be genuinely enthusiastic

If you have given your testimony well, the listener walks away knowing what God has done in your life and what He can do in theirs.

Chapter Eighteen

Let's Look at a Sample Testimony

One of the most effective ways of giving an evangelistic message in a church or workplace setting is through your own story. A non-Christian may argue with what the Bible says, but he or she cannot argue with what has happened to you. Here is my own five-minute testimony succinctly stated. I've broken it down with the three parts of an effective testimony so that you know how your own testimony needs to be developed.

Part 1: Before I trusted Christ, this is how I thought and lived.

Using a strong opening statement, explain how you used to think about God, the Bible, life, etc. Don't try to explain everything, but give a few details to try to explain where you were both spiritually and mentally.

Before I came to Christ, I thought that in order to get to heaven, I had to be good and do the best that I could. So I went to church each Sunday and often read my Bible. But the question I had was, "How will I know when I am good enough to get to heaven?"

Part 2: Here is how I came to understand the gospel and trust Christ.

Here again are the four parts that need to be stressed. Explain how you came to understand these four truths.

We are sinners.

I grew up on a dairy farm in Pennsylvania, and I've always loved creation. On Sunday afternoons as a teenager, I would go out to my dad's twelve-acre patch of woods and spend hours just sitting under a tree. As I looked at the squirrels, the trees, and the clouds, I would think of God and spiritual things. Dad was a hunter and taught me how to hunt. That time in the outdoors made me think more of God and more of spiritual things. I decided to study the Bible. At first, I thought it was both boring and confusing. But I kept reading and studying and learned something that I never knew.

As part of a hard-working and moral family, I saw myself as a good person. With my responsibilities on the farm, I did not have time to get into trouble. We got up at five o'clock every morning and worked hard all day. Before I started reading the Bible, I never saw myself as a sinner. When I compared myself to many people, I thought I looked pretty good. I thought that because I was a good person, I would go to heaven. Then I read statements in the Bible such as, "For all have sinned and fall short of the glory of God." I realized that no matter how good I'd been, I had not been perfect. The standard was not other people, but the perfection of God. I had unkind thoughts, selfish actions, and fits of anger just like everybody else did. I came to understand that when God looked at me, He did not see me as a good, moral person. Instead, He saw me as a sinner.

The penalty of sin is death.

Seeing myself as a sinner was one thing. Recognizing the penalty for that sin was another. As I studied the Bible, I came to see that God is more than simply a good God. God is a holy God. And being a holy

God, He has no choice but to punish sin. And the punishment for my sin was death. It did not matter how hard I'd tried; my efforts would not change my eternal future. In many ways, I felt frustrated because here I was, a sinner, and no matter how much good I had done, it would not make up for what I had done wrong.

Christ died for us and rose again.

Now you must understand that since our family went to church every Sunday, I always heard that Christ died for my sins. But I thought you went to heaven by being good and doing the best that you could. I did not understand that He died for me. He was my substitute. On the cross, where they should have hung me, they punished Him. The third day He rose again, proving that He had conquered sin and the grave.

We can be saved through faith.

Here is the one thing that for so many years I missed. I felt like most people do—the way you get to heaven was by going to church, doing good, living right. What I failed to realize was that because Jesus Christ died for my sins and rose again, eternal life was free because He had already paid the price. That's when I found out the truth of this Bible verse: "The wages of sin is death, but the gift of God is eternal life in Christ Jesus our Lord." So then my question was, "How do I receive that gift?" One word in the Bible I kept seeing over and over again was the word believe. *For example, Jesus Christ said, "I am the resurrection and the life. He who believes in Me, though he may die, he shall live. And whoever lives and believes in Me shall never die." I came to understand that believe means to trust, to depend on, to rely on. As a sinner, I had to put my trust in Jesus Christ alone as my only way to heaven—not Christ and my good works, but Christ alone as my only way to heaven. One night in my early teens, I knelt by my bed on the dairy farm and I trusted Jesus Christ as my personal Savior and received His free gift of eternal life. Looking back, I now realize that on that night, God took me from the creation to the Creator to Christ.*

Part 3: After I trusted Christ,
this is how my life changed.

Help the listener see how your life has changed. Again, don't try to explain everything, but give a few details that help your hearer understand. As you close, summarize your testimony into one sentence that captures your story from beginning to end.

To explain to you how my life has changed would take a book, not a paragraph. But the greatest thing that has happened is that I know beyond any doubt that if I were to die, I would go straight to heaven. I don't have to worry about dying unexpectedly. I no longer have to fear death. I used to fear death so much I imagined what every member of my family would look like if they were lying in a coffin. I thought about death a lot. Now I know that when life on earth ends, life in the presence of Christ will begin. I found out through my own study of the Bible, which is how I came to Christ, that being good would not get me to heaven. What God wanted was for me to trust Christ as my only way to heaven. I know that when I die, I will be with Christ. And while I am living, He, as a real Person, will be with me. And it doesn't matter what problems come into my life, what temptations I face, what disappointments I suffer, He and I will face them together. Several years ago, I fell off a ladder and broke my heel. Lying in bed for two weeks before I could even move was not something I thought I could ever endure. But Christ was right there helping me one day at a time.

I would summarize my testimony in this way. I found out through my own study of the Bible that religion could take me to church, but only Jesus Christ could take me to heaven. The day I trusted Christ was the greatest day of my life and the greatest decision I ever made.

Part 7

Resources for
Workplace Leaders

Chapter Nineteen

How Can Workplace Leaders Learn Evangelistic Speaking?

This section is especially for workplace leaders—those who are often called upon to make presentations, to address groups of employees, or are invited to speak to civic, fraternal, or community organizations. While not every person in the workplace will have opportunities to speak before groups on a regular basis, it is almost part of the job description for the workplace leader. While workplace leaders know how to speak about their particular area of expertise, they may not always feel as comfortable taking advantage of wider opportunities.

Here's a simple thought exercise: name the first ten professions that come to your mind. Immediately you may think: doctor, lawyer, dentist, business professional, teacher, electrician, carpenter, salesman, engineer, and law enforcement. Generally, the professions that come to mind first are often your own occupation and those of people close to you.

What do all of those occupations have in common? The answer is obvious. They all require know-how. Before you can enter any profession or trade, you must—even if it's through self-study and experience—gain the know-how.

Now let's go a step further and ask, "Where did the know-how come from?" Here is where the answers vary. An insurance salesman who is a close friend of mine taught his son and son-in-law the business. My doctor friend learned his skills in medical school and through an internship. A carpenter friend learned largely through self-study combining books and experience. None of these escaped the need for know-how.

Know-how is essential in evangelistic speaking. Where and how do workplace leaders learn how to speak evangelistically? It's not usually where church leaders learned it—in a Bible college or seminary classroom. Nor is it always through the same place. Any combination of resources can be used to teach workplace leaders how to speak, and in particular, how to speak evangelistically.

It begins with passion and desire.

It's easy to overlook the obvious when it comes to learning how to speak. Resources are abundant, but effective speaking starts with passion and desire. In fact, I would suggest that a speaker not even examine the resources unless he or she has that passion and desire to speak. A speaker's enjoyment and passion shows regardless of the topic he addresses. Whenever I listen to a good speaker, I sense there is something he is deeply burdened about. When the passion is there, we will seek the resources we need and not give up until we find them. If the passion to speak is not there, the resources don't matter.

Use professional organizations.

There are professional organizations dedicated to teaching speaking. One is Toastmasters International. They have had a worldwide influence in helping people become more competent and comfortable in front of an audience. With members in more than ninety different countries, they help would-be speakers develop and improve their skills in speaking. Done in an enjoyable, positive, and fun-filled way in a small group setting, their teaching prepares speakers for both impromptu and prepared speech presentations.

Use educational institutions.

If a university, Bible college, or seminary is nearby, review their curriculum. Sometimes they will offer classes on public speaking as a service to the public. Keep in mind that Bible college or seminary classes might be more focused on teaching or speaking in a Christian environment. Often, however, principles taught for speaking in a Christian environment can be adapted to evangelistic speaking in the workplace. As I've noted several times, evangelistic speaking is speaking. Some classes obviously are more beneficial than others, depending on both the professor and the content. But a principle or two given in a class can make a profound difference in developing speaking skills. Principles learned through numerous classes add up.

Read books.

I have nearly fifty books on speaking in my library. Because of my profession, most of them focus on preaching. At the same time, principles of communication taught in some of those books would help any speaker in the workplace. For example, a book written by Dr. Haddon Robinson that discusses the "Big Idea" approach to putting together a sermon will show you the importance of the same approach in putting together a workplace message.

Books about speaking are not the only books I have in mind. Books on leadership have also been helpful to me and would be helpful to any workplace speaker. For example, John Maxwell's *The 21 Irrefutable Laws of Leadership* is a favorite of mine. Chapter 10 of that book discusses the law of communication. Maxwell explains that leaders should touch a heart before they ask for a hand. What he says in that chapter about the importance of emotion, and even about addressing large groups as individuals, would help any evangelistic speaker.

A third category of books is titles that focus on faith in the workplace. One I'd recommend is *Going Public with Your Faith* by William Peel and Walt Larimore. Their discussion of how to be a spiritual influence at work is one of the best I've read. Everything they share has to do with personal evangelism. Nevertheless, principles on balancing truth with grace and knowledge with humility that are taught in the book are equally important in evangelistic speaking. For example, the authors comment, "Grace calls for the kind of compassion that points people to the One who can meet their needs."[1] If that grace is not evident in our public speaking, we are unlikely to draw sinners to Christ.

When considering books that will help you develop your evangelistic speaking skills, don't ask, "Is this about evangelistic speaking?" Ask instead, "Is this about speaking, leadership, or workplace evangelism?" Since all involve communication, any book with solid instruction in those areas is likely to give you some know-how in evangelistic speaking.

Listen to communicators.

Whom do you know who communicates well to an audience? Listen to them every opportunity you have. Then ask, "What are they doing that could help me in speaking evangelistically in the workplace?" For example, humor is essential in evangelistic speaking. Any good communicator, regardless of his audience, has learned the importance of humor. If a person uses humor effectively, watch how he begins and ends his humor. His audience may be believers or unbelievers. Either way, you will be helped in your own use of humor by watching someone else.

Don't limit yourself to Christian communicators. Secular speakers are often good communicators, even though at times they communicate the wrong thing. Observing their ability to get an idea across has sometimes helped me enhance my own ability. Even what they do wrong teaches me. One speaker I heard recently was most difficult to listen to. His pride overshadowed everything he said. It made me leave wanting to be careful that pride does not creep into my own presentations. On the other hand, his effective use of stories and analogies would have helped any evangelistic speaker.

Get experience.

God directs a moving object. Know-how comes from taking what you do know and doing something with it. A person who has spoken five times is better off than the one who has never spoken.

I spoke at a luncheon made up of 80 percent non-Christians. For numerous reasons, I felt I did poorly at this particular event. As I reflected on it, I realized that my problem was the way I had approached my material. I should have started where I ended. One time doing it wrong was all it took to learn how to do it right.

Don't concern yourself with the "size" of the speaking opportunity. A chance to say something in front of twenty people can be great preparation for saying it in front of two hundred people. When God develops know-how in us, He does it a step at a time. Such an opportunity could be a first step that leads to an even larger one and enhances your comfort and confidence before an audience.

The adage "There is no substitute for experience" fits here. Gain as much experience as you can. Know-how comes through experience.

KEY POINTS

Know-how isn't difficult to obtain. Developing know-how in evangelistic speaking comes through:

- Passion and desire
- Using professional organizations
- Using educational institutions
- Reading books on speaking, leadership, and evangelism
- Listening to communicators
- Obtaining experience

Some important aspects of evangelistic speaking are learned more quickly than others. But learning comes through multiple resources, not just one.

Chapter Twenty

Speaking Opportunities for Workplace Leaders

An experience of a lifetime! A commercial airline pilot friend called and said, "Larry, if you and Tammy can come right now, I can take you through the new flight simulator at DFW Airport." We didn't need a second invitation. I piloted the "virtual plane" into various airports, under varying weather conditions, during daylight and dark. Never have I been so grateful for an experience. Never have I been so grateful it wasn't a real plane! I remember one of his instructions. "Don't touch this button," he warned. He showed me how it would send the plane into a nosedive. Pointing to the other controls he said, "You may touch these." Changing one control setting would result in a catastrophe on a real flight.

In evangelistic speaking, there is a "don't touch" button. There is something we can't and don't dare change: the gospel message. That gospel is defined in 1 Corinthians 15:3–4 and can be reduced to ten words: Christ died for our sins and rose from the dead. That gospel is so close to God's heart that He gives a severe warning to whoever might tamper with it. The apostle Paul, writing in Galatians 1:8, warns: "But even if we, or an angel from heaven, preach any other gospel to you than what we have preached to you, let him be accursed." That phrase "let him be accursed" is one of the strongest declarations used by the apostle Paul. To be "accursed" means to be under the discipline of God.

However, there is another "button" that we can and must engage. It's the means by which we communicate the gospel message. When it comes to an evangelistic message in the workplace, the means can vary greatly.

I cannot stress enough the importance of an evangelistic mindset. If we have an evangelistic outlook, we can think of more ways evangelistic messages can be given than this chapter could ever address. All we need is a mind that consistently thinks about unbelievers and their need of Christ.

To stimulate your thinking, the following are several different types of evangelistic messages workplace leaders can give. Let's start with one that is the most common as well as one that is the most effective.

Personal Testimony

As mentioned earlier, I may argue with what you say. I may dispute what you believe. But I cannot argue with what has happened to you. Your testimony, effectively delivered, can play a big part in causing me to consider spiritual things and particularly my own need of Christ. That testimony may be delivered in a wide range of venues. You may deliver it at a luncheon given in your honor to recognize the contributions you've made to your employer. You might share it at a company holiday celebration or an outreach luncheon sponsored by a business or church.

Some time ago, I spoke at a luncheon where a workplace leader gave her testimony. It was riveting. Years earlier, she and her girlfriends attended a party and came under the influence of alcohol. Driving home drunk, she failed to turn a sharp corner and her two girlfriends were killed. She lived with that guilt until she trusted Christ and found forgiveness. Her testimony, used of the Holy Spirit, resulted in people in the workplace coming to Christ.

Testimonies shaped into evangelistic messages are effective. A testimony used as an evangelistic message must not only explain how you came to Christ, it must also tell me how your listeners can come to Christ as well.

After-Dinner Speeches

If testimonies are the most effective opportunities for evangelistic speaking, after-dinner speeches are next. In referring to them as "after-dinner" speeches, I mean a message given at any kind of meal setting. I've seen these used at numerous business luncheons where believers are encouraged to bring non-Christian acquaintances. Whatever is promoted, acquaintances should be invited with a "front door" approach. In other words, the non-Christians should fully understand what they are attending. Trickery is not honoring to God nor does it help the non-Christian.

A workplace leader who gives an after-dinner message has a superb opportunity. Her workplace experience gives her credibility. Her ability to communicate takes those who have just had a physical meal and causes them to reflect upon spiritual food that comes straight from the Scriptures. Such after-dinner speaking opportunities may be at a men-only or women-only gathering. They can present an opportunity to give your testimony as an evangelistic message. Stonecroft Ministries has used such testimonies for years at their outreach luncheons.

Another kind of after-dinner speaking opportunity may be one where you address a topic such as "If you have to be good to get to heaven, how good is good enough?" Topics like this are particularly effective when it is announced ahead of time that such a question will be addressed. Remember, we are not trying to trick non-Christians. These after-dinner speeches may also address particular topics of interest to non-Christians such as mentoring, prioritizing, money management, success, time management, loneliness, or boredom. It may even be an after-dinner message given at a "Celebrate America" occasion close to Independence Day on July 4th. An evangelistic message could give a historical approach to the freedom the early Pilgrims sought. Part of that freedom was the religious freedom to worship God as they pleased, a topic that provides an opportunity to clearly and boldly explain the gospel.

In a largely unmotivated society, motivational speeches seem to be the order of the day. They may center on anything from "How to Motivate Yourself" to "How to Motivate Your Children." A friend of mine recently spoke to workplace CEOs on "How to Motivate Your Employees." Some of these speaking opportunities may not allow for an evangelistic message; others do. Even if you can't give an invitation to come to Christ, you might be able to give an example from Scripture. For example, how did Jesus Christ, the greatest Person who ever lived, motivate people? Second Corinthians 5:14–15 tells us. Paul declared, "For the love of Christ compels us, because we judge thus: that if One died for all, then all died; and He died for all, that those who live should live no longer for themselves, but for Him who died for them and rose again." Christ motivates us by His love for us. That love was proven by His death on the cross on our behalf and His resurrection. Such a message can explain the gospel even when it is not fitting to invite the audience to receive it.

Whatever the topic, it is important that the transition to the gospel is both smooth and natural. For example, to say, "The answer to boredom is Christ," is not natural or truthful. I know committed Christians who are often bored. But to say, "Knowing Christ makes life bearable when it tends to be boring," is both natural and truthful. If the transition is unnatural, the speaker senses it and even more importantly, so do the lost people who are listening.

A word of caution—Don't sensationalize the gospel or present something that is unbiblical. For example, the promise behind the gospel is life in the hereafter that is the happiest and most fulfilling it's ever been. Nowhere does God ever promise health and wealth to those who come to Christ. The gospel is about heavenly pardon, not earthly prosperity.

Retreat Messages

Retreats offer some of the most direct evangelistic opportunities. Largely made up of people from the workplace, those who attend retreats often have been sensitized to spiritual things. A series of messages allows a workplace leader to "build" his messages in such a way that upon the conclusion of the retreat, a direct appeal is made to come to Christ. Church leaders often give messages at such retreats. However, workplace leaders who are good communicators as well as students of the Scriptures can also give such messages. A friend of mine who is a leader in the workplace and a committed Christian serves as a CPA. He welcomes opportunities to speak at retreats. His knowledge of the Word makes his messages comparable to sermons even though he's a workplace leader, not a church leader.

Commencement Addresses

Workplace leaders often make very effective speakers for commencement addresses for high schools or colleges. Because they are respected in the community, they can give a needed challenge to students in areas such as hard work, integrity, community service, etc. Commencement addresses also enable the speaker to explain how his relationship with Christ has impacted everything he does. Not only is the graduating class impacted with the gospel, but family members and friends of the graduates are impacted as well.

We have been blessed by the Internet. Type in "commencement address" and note all the suggestions that appear. A workplace leader can take any of these and ask, "Would this allow me to give an evangelistic twist to it?"

Eulogies

This has to be one of the most overlooked opportunities. When a person dies, a friend in the workplace is often asked to give a eulogy. To fail to use such an occasion when death is foremost on everyone's mind is to neglect a great opportunity. We must be careful to avoid "pushing" people into a decision for Christ right then and there. I have found those opportunities so overloaded with emotion that we must take care that people are making an intelligent decision to come to Christ, not just an emotional one. An effective eulogy will give details of the person's life, along with special memories that family and friends have. Don't hesitate to use humor, especially if the person was known for his sense of humor. Include statements the person made and things he did that benefitted others. Be sure your eulogy has a flow to it, whether it is chronological or topic-driven such as his family and work. Don't lose your audience by confusing dates, events, and times. Ultimately, you want to end up emphasizing, "The most important thing your friend and my friend (mentioning name) would want you to know is . . ." Then if the person was a believer, boldly explain the gospel. Make clear what all need to know: (1) we are all sinners, (2) Christ died for our sins and rose again, and (3) we must trust Christ.

What if the person was not a believer? The truth cannot be denied, nor can a misrepresentation occur here. This is also not the time to focus on where that person is—forever separated from God. What a eulogy can do is focus on who the person was and any achievements he made, the things everyone liked about him, etc. The transition can then be, "But let's not just focus on his passing. Let's focus on ours, because sooner than we think, we will all face our own death. So we ought to ask a question—not where is (the deceased), but where would I be?" Then give the gospel clearly and invite each one to settle the matter of his or her own eternal destiny before the day is over. Sometimes people can be encouraged to trust Christ during a moment of silent meditation at the funeral or in the privacy of their own home. Many will often come to Christ as a result of a funeral instead of at the funeral. Regardless, each person should leave knowing that the moment he places his trust in Christ alone as his only way to heaven, he is forever His.

KEY POINTS

A workplace leader is limited by his message when it comes to the gospel. No changes allowed. That message is, Christ died for our sins and rose from the dead. However, he's not limited by the kind of message he can give that allows him to present that message. Occasions are:

- Personal testimony
- After-dinner speeches
- Retreat messages
- Commencement addresses
- Eulogies

When effectively done, such messages take a person from where he is to where he needs to be—in a right relationship with Jesus Christ.

Chapter Twenty-One

Let's Look at a Sample Message for Workplace Leaders

This is the kind of message that is suitable for a friendship dinner sponsored by a church. It's also one that could be given at certain workplace settings where the speaker is given the freedom to address anything of his choosing. The advantage of a title like this is that it answers a question non-Christians have since they often find the Bible very confusing. It even demonstrates how you can take an idea or two the Bible gives and develop a talk around it. Just be sure you are giving the meaning the Bible gives so as not to misuse or abuse the Scripture. Topics like this are very effective in some workplace situations and can be given by anyone with speaking ability. Bible college or seminary training is not required.

Title: Since the Bible is so confusing, is there anything it says the average person can understand?

Main idea: The two things nobody can misunderstand are: the wages of sin is death but the gift of God is eternal life through Jesus Christ our Lord.

We have them every single day. Sometimes with a friend. Sometimes with a foe. With someone so special as our kids and with someone so specialized as our mechanic. But we have them every single day.

I'm referring to conversations. Conversations with a neighbor; conversations with a niece. With a parent; with a peer. In the midst of those conversations, statements are made that could fit into one of three categories: statements we cannot understand, statements we only think we understand, and statements we cannot misunderstand. Let's talk about those three for a minute.

First, people make statements we cannot understand. Two kinds of people have an international reputation for speaking in such a way we cannot understand them. One is called a politician and the other is called a preacher. They are so difficult to understand that they may remind you of Christopher Columbus—when he started out he didn't know where he was going; when he got there, he didn't know where he was; when he came back, he didn't know where he had been!

One time, some concerned parents were talking to their child's teacher about his progress. They said, "We cannot read his handwriting." The teacher said, "That's no problem. That means he is going to be a doctor." The parents said, "But we don't even understand him when he talks." The teacher said, "That is a problem. That means he's going to be a politician."

By the same token, there was a preacher who was so difficult to understand that people endured his messages instead of enjoying them and often fell asleep while he was speaking. Someone asked a church member, "What color are your pastor's eyes?" He answered. "I have no idea. When he prays, he closes his eyes. When he preaches, I close mine."

Then, there are those statements we only think we understand. Now sometimes that's because of a poor choice of words on the part of the person doing the talking. Reader's Digest told the story of a woman and her two children who were fishing in the Alaskan wilderness. Her husband was about one hundred yards downstream. Suddenly a baby moose wandered out of the brush. The children ran up to it, and hugged and kissed it. All of a sudden, Mama Moose came out of the brush. Her head was lowered, her ears were up, her nostrils were flaring, and she was ready to charge. The mother ran between Mama Moose and her children, waved her hands back and forth, and yelled until her throat was raw. Mama Moose took one look at the mother and went back in the brush. That night, the little boy told his dad about it. He said to his dad, "You should have been there. Mommy scared this big moose away with nothing but her face."

Finally, there are statements we cannot misunderstand. Sometimes they are encouraging. Sometimes they are discouraging. Sometimes they are an inspiration. Sometimes they are an insult. But you cannot misunderstand them. As you may remember, Sir Winston Churchill's friendship with the wealthy and sharp-tongued Lady Astor was a cat and dog kind of relationship. One of their most famous exchanges was:

Lady Astor: "Winston, if you were my husband, I'd poison your tea."

Churchill: "Nancy, if I were your husband, I'd drink it."

There are statements we cannot understand, statements we only think we understand, and statements we cannot misunderstand. In that connection, it is interesting that nine out of ten Americans say they own a copy of the Bible. But less than half spend any time reading it. And the main reason they give is that it's so confusing they do not understand it.

Now, I can identify. There are books in the Bible called epistles and there are men in the Bible called apostles. When I first read the Bible, I thought perhaps an epistle was the wife of an apostle. That made sense to me. Here's Mr. Apostle and here's his wife Mrs. Epistle. So that raises the question: since the Bible is so confusing, is there anything it says that normal people can understand?

Although I would admit that there are some things in the Bible we do not understand and some things in the Bible we probably only think we understand, there are at least two things the Bible says that we cannot misunderstand. And these are the two most important things the Bible has to say. The first is something no one wants to hear, and the second is something everyone needs to hear.

The first thing the Bible says that no one can misunderstand is that the wages of sin is death. The reason we don't like to hear that is that no one likes to think of himself or herself as a sinner. More often than we care to admit, we're like the man whose success had gone to his head and he compared himself to past and present greats like John D. Rockefeller and Bill Gates. So he said to his wife, "Do you realize how many great businessmen there are in the world today?" She said, "No, but there's one less than you think."

The Bible does not say we are great people. Instead, we are sinners. The word *sin* in the Bible means "to miss the mark." I once met a woman who had an intense desire to be an airline flight attendant. But at that time the regulations required a flight attendant to be at least five foot two inches tall. She was five foot one. It did not matter how good or honest she was. She had missed the mark.

Similarly, God has set a standard for getting to heaven. He says you must be perfect. But it doesn't matter how religiously we live, how good we are, or how hard we try. We cannot be as perfect as God demands. All of us are sinners. And the problem is that God, being the holy God He is, has to punish sin, and therefore He has declared, "The wages of sin is death."

You and I like to make excuses for what we do wrong and not accept responsibility for it. I'm sure you have read the statements some people give when they are in a car accident and don't want to accept the responsibility for it. They are hilarious. Here are some of my favorites:

"The pedestrian had no idea which way to go so I ran over him."
"The guy was all over the road. I had to swerve a number of times before I hit him."

"A truck backed through the windshield into my wife's face."

"The cause of the accident was a little guy in a small car with a big mouth."

"I pulled over to the side of the road, glanced at my in-laws, and ran over the embankment."

But here's my very favorite:

"Coming home, I drove into the wrong driveway and collided with a tree I did not know I had."

God cannot excuse sin. It is punishable by death. Death is one of those things we don't like to think about, but we do. In fact, a university survey revealed that, next to sex, the main thing on the minds of young people today is death. The fear of death is something we live with every day. A philosopher once said, "Adults fear death like children fear the dark." It has also been said, "The fear of death does not keep us from dying. It just keeps us from living." Frankly, if death were just physical, it wouldn't be so bad. But when the Bible says, "The wages of sin is death," it means that we deserve to die physically and be separated from God forever.

I know what you are thinking. "Larry, you have to be the most exciting after-dinner speaker I've ever heard. Everything you've said is bad news. If I wanted bad news, I could have stayed home and stared at my bank account."

But there is not just one thing the Bible says that cannot be misunderstood—there are two things. The second thing is as encouraging as the first thing is discouraging.

The second thing the Bible says that no one can misunderstand is, "But the gift of God is eternal life through Jesus Christ our Lord."

We often say, "Nothing in life is free," and quite frankly, that's just not true. One Christmas season, a post office in Troy, Michigan, called a couple in Detroit and told them there was a forty-pound package waiting for them sent from a man who had their same last name. They had no idea who he was but assumed it was a relative they did not know they had. Excited to no end, they went to the post office, picked up the package, and began driving home. As they were driving, they said to each other, "This could be a joke. Or worse, that thing could be a bomb!" So they called the post office, which in turn called the bomb squad. They took the package to a remote island and blew it to bits. When the ashes settled, all that was left were portions of a factory invoice and guarantee for a brand new stereo system that was indeed being sent to them by a relative they did not know they had. Some things in life are free. And the Bible says that eternal life is a completely free gift.

But you are probably saying, "How can it be free? I've always heard that you have to work your way to heaven." As a man once said, "I always figured the harder you worked, the higher you went."

But have you ever thought how much of our confusion could be removed if we would just ask questions as simple as we used to ask when we were little. I love the story a national magazine told of some Cub Scouts visiting the Cincinnati office of the FBI. When they stopped to view mug shots of the Ten Most Wanted men in the United States, one little boy pointed to a picture and asked if that really was the most wanted person. The FBI man assured him that, yes, that was his actual photograph. The boy then asked, "Then why didn't you keep him when you took his picture?"

A lot of our confusion could be resolved with a question so simple as "why?"

If you were to ask God how He gives eternal life as a gift, He would answer in five words: through Jesus Christ our Lord. By that He means that Jesus Christ, the perfect Son of God, came into the world and He took your sin and my sin and placed it upon Himself. He died in our place on a cross. He was crucified when we should have been crucified.

A number of years ago, a man requested in his will that when he died he be cremated and his ashes spread over the Atlantic Ocean at the spot where the *Titanic* sank in 1912. He had been on that ship with his parents that cold April night. When boarding the lifeboat, there was only room for two more. His father gently carried him to the edge of the ship and lowered the boy and his mother into the lifeboat. The father died that night. He went down with the *Titanic*. The boy never forgot watching the ship submerge in the distance. But that dad saved his family by dying for them. He died in their place.

The Bible tells us that Jesus Christ came into the world, took your sin and my sin, placed it upon Himself, and died in our place. The reason that eternal life is a free gift is because Christ already paid the price. He died for our sins and rose again the third day.

The Statue of Liberty in New York Harbor was a gift from France in 1876 to celebrate our one hundredth anniversary as a nation. Although it did not cost America anything, it cost France much. The citizens of France raised money to pay for it out of their own pockets. It was free to us because the price had already been paid. Eternal life is free because the price has already been paid by Jesus Christ. God simply asks us to come to Him as a sinner, recognize Christ died for us and rose again, and trust in Christ alone as our only way to heaven. That's why Christ said in John 6:47, "He who believes in Me has everlasting life." That word *believe* means "to trust, depend, rely on."

One time in northern Quebec on the Broadbeck River, three fishermen were canoeing when a storm arose. The strong and damaging winds overturned the small boat. Though the canoe sank, an ice chest that had been cooling their cokes floated to the top of the water. They battled the rushing current but soon realized they could not save themselves. So they pulled that ice chest under them, rested their weight upon it, and trusted it to save them. And it did. They believed in it.

God asks us to come to Him as sinners, recognize Christ died for us and rose again, and put our trust in Christ alone as our only way to heaven—not depending on our good life to save us, our baptism, our church attendance, or the sacraments we've taken, but trusting Christ alone as our only way to heaven. The moment we do, God gives us eternal life as a gift.

My point is, there are some things in the Bible we don't understand. There are some things in the Bible we only think we understand. But there are two things the Bible says that we cannot misunderstand. These two things are: The wages of sin is death, but the gift of God is eternal life through Jesus Christ our Lord.

Mark Twain once said, "The parts of the Bible that bother me the most are not the parts I don't understand. It's those I do." Don't worry about the parts of the Bible you don't understand. Worry about the parts you do.

So to answer our original question: since the Bible is so confusing, does it say anything that normal people can understand? The answer is yes: (1) The wages of sin is death, (2) but the gift of God is eternal life through Jesus Christ our Lord.

Some time ago, I read something distressing. The *Dallas Morning News* told of a conversation with one of the richest men in America in which he admitted that sooner or later, every one of our lives comes to an end. And he made the honest confession that he is convinced we go someplace. But he said, "I cannot for the life of me figure out where." That tells me he has never read the two statements of the Bible that cannot be misunderstood. Because those two statements answer the question of where—either life with God or separation from God. For that reason, if people want to know where they are going when they die, they don't need to ask, "What will He do with me?" They only need to ask, "What have I done with Him?"

As you are aware, American Express advertised their services and products throughout the world with one simple slogan. It was so well known, you still remember it. If I start it, you can finish it. It goes like this—"American Express, don't [leave home without it]." Some time ago, someone came up with a great improvement on that slogan that has a lot more significance and meaning—"Jesus Christ, don't leave earth without Him."

As your friend at this Friendship Dinner, I want to encourage you—don't leave earth without Him. Because the wages of sin is death, but the gift of God is eternal life through Jesus Christ our Lord.

may I ask you a question

Has anyone
ever taken
a Bible and
shown you
how you can
know for sure
that you're going
to heaven?

The Bible contains both **bad news** and **good news**. The *bad news* is something about **YOU**. The *good news* is something about **GOD**.

Let's look at the bad news first...

Bad News 1

We are all sinners.
Romans 3:23 says, *"For all have sinned and fall short of the glory of God."*

"Sinned" means that we have missed the mark. When we lie, hate, lust, or gossip, we have missed the standard God has set.

Suppose you and I were each to throw a rock and try to hit the North Pole. You might throw farther than I, but neither of us would hit it.

When the Bible says "All have sinned and fall short," it means that we have all come short of God's standard of perfection.

In thoughts, words, and deeds, we have not been perfect.

But the bad news gets worse...

Bad News 2

The penalty for sin is death.

Romans 6:23 says, *"For the wages of sin is death."*

Suppose you worked for me and I paid you $50. That $50 was your wages. That's what you earned.

The Bible says that by sinning we have earned death. That means we deserve to die and be separated from God forever.

Since there was no way we could come to God, the Bible says that _God came to us!_

Good News 1

Christ died for you.
Romans 5:8 says, *"But God demonstrates His own love toward us, in that while we were still sinners, Christ died for us."*

Suppose you are in a hospital dying of cancer. I come to you and say, "Let's take the cancer cells from **your** body and put them into **my** body."

If that were possible,
What would happen to me?
What would happen to you?

I would die and you would live.

I would die in your place.

The Bible says Christ took the penalty that we deserved for sin, placed it upon Himself, and *died in our place.* Three days later Christ came back to life to prove that sin and death had been conquered and that His claims to be God were true.

Just as the bad news got worse, the good news gets better!

Good News 2

You can be saved through faith in Christ.

Ephesians 2:8-9 says, *"For by grace [undeserved favor] you have been saved [delivered from sin's penalty] through faith, and that not of yourselves; it is the gift of God, not of works, lest anyone should boast."*

Faith means *trust.*

Q. What must you trust Christ for?
A. You must depend on Him alone to forgive you and to give you eternal life.

Just as you trust a chair to hold you through no effort of your own, *so you must trust Jesus Christ to get you to heaven* through no effort of your own.

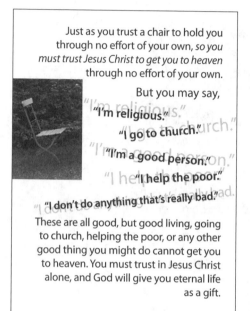

But you may say,

"I'm religious."

"I go to church."

"I'm a good person."

"I help the poor."

"I don't do anything that's really bad."

These are all good, but good living, going to church, helping the poor, or any other good thing you might do cannot get you to heaven. You must trust in Jesus Christ alone, and God will give you eternal life as a gift.

Is there anything keeping you from trusting Christ right now?

1. _____

2. _____

3. _____

4. _____

Think carefully. There is nothing more important than your need to trust Christ.

Would you like to tell God you are **trusting Jesus Christ as your Savior?** If you would, why not pray right now and tell God you are trusting His Son?

Remember!

It is not a prayer that saves you. It is trusting Jesus Christ that saves you. Prayer is simply how you tell God what you are doing.

Dear God, I know I'm a sinner. I know my sin deserves to be punished. I believe Christ died for me and rose from the grave. I trust Jesus Christ alone as my Savior. Thank You for the forgiveness and everlasting life I now have. In Jesus' name, amen.

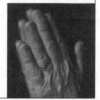

What just happened?

John 5:24 explains, *"He who hears My word and believes in Him who sent Me has everlasting life, and shall not come into judgment, but has passed from death into life."*

» Did you **"hear"** God's word?
» Did you **"believe"** what God said and trust Christ as your Savior?
» Does **"has everlasting life"** mean later or right now?
» Does it say **"shall not come into judgment"** or **might not**?
» Does it say **"has passed from death"** or **shall pass**?

Eternal life is based on fact, not feeling.

Memorize John 5:24 today.

What do you do now?

Having trusted Christ as your only way to heaven, here's how to **grow** in your relationship with Him.

» Tell God what's on your mind through prayer (Philippians 4:6,7).

» Read the Bible daily, to learn more about Him and learn from Him (2 Timothy 3:16,17). Start in the book of Philippians.

» Worship with God's people in a local church (Hebrews 10:24,25).

» Tell others about Jesus Christ (Matthew 4:19).

If you have found this booklet helpful, please share it with someone else. If you have further questions about what is contained in this booklet, contact:

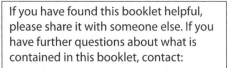

The Gospel. Clear and Simple.®

p.o. box 741417 | dallas, tx 75374
www.evantell.org | 800.947.7359
© 2012 evantell, inc.   TRMEN004

Notes

Introduction
1. Haddon Robinson, Doctorate of Ministry Residency (lecture, Gordon-Conwell Theological Seminary, Hamilton, MA, August, 2006).

Chapter One
1. While this statement isn't found in Luther's own writings, it is widely attributed to him.

Chapter Two
1. Lewis Sperry Chafer, *True Evangelism* (Grand Rapids: Dunham, 1973), 71.
2. Quoted in *Our Daily Bread*, September 1992.

Chapter Four
1. Quoted in *Our Daily Bread*, January 2002.

Chapter Five
1. Randy Kilgore, *Talking About God in the Twenty-First Century Marketplace* (Boston: Marketplace Network, Inc., 2003), 72.
2. Quoted in Milburn H. Miller, *Notes and Quotes for Church Speakers* (Anderson, IN: Warner, 1960), 186.

Chapter Eight
1. Quoted in *Our Daily Bread*, December 1984.
2. Quoted in *Our Daily Bread*, November-December 1984.

Chapter Nine

1. Warren Wiersbe and David Wiersbe, *The Elements of Preaching* (Wheaton, IL: Tyndale House, 1986), 78.

2. Douglas Groothuis, "The Gnostic Jesus," Christian Research Institute (excerpted from article DG040-1 of the *Christian Research Journal*), accessed January 8, 2012, www.equip.org/articles/the-gnostic-jesus.

3. "That they said (in boast), 'We killed Christ Jesus the son of Mary, the Messenger of Allah'; but they killed him not, nor crucified him, but so it was made to appear to them, and those who differ therein are full of doubts, with no (certain) knowledge, but only conjecture to follow, for of a surety they killed him not: Nay, Allah raised him up unto Himself; and Allah is Exalted in Power, Wise" (Qur'an 4:157–158).

4. Wilbur M. Smith, *Therefore Stand: Christian Apologetics* (Grand Rapids: Baker, 1972), 425.

5. Quoted by Ewen Huffman, "The Empty Tomb: What Does It Mean?" added March 2002, http://www.sermoncentral.com/sermon.asp?SermonID=45057.

6. Henry M. Morris, "The Resurrection of Christ—The Best-Proved Fact in History," Institute for Creation Research (adapted from *Many Infallible Proofs* [San Diego: Master Books, 1974]), accessed March 20, 2012, http://www.icr.org/ChristResurrection/.

Chapter Ten

1. Dreama Turkett, "All in a Day's Work," *Reader's Digest* (July 2005): 53.

2. Don Zaidle, "Killer Cougars," *Outdoor Life* (February 2001): 46–47; available at http://www.outdoorlife.com/articles/hunting/2007/09/killer-cougars.

Chapter Eleven

1. Lewis Sperry Chafer, *Systematic Theology*, vols. 3 and 4 (Dallas Theological Seminary, 1948; Grand Rapids: Kregel, 1976), 376.

2. A third word, *metemelomai*, carries the sense of "to regret" and is only used six times in the New Testament. It is used only once in a salvation-related context.

3. William Evans, *The Great Doctrines of the Bible*, rev. ed. (1912; Chicago: Moody Press, 1949), 140.

Chapter Fourteen

1. Quoted by Robert D. Foster, *The Navigator: Dawson Trotman* (Colorado Springs: NavPress, 1983), 123.
2. Dawson Trotman, *Born to Reproduce* (Colorado Springs: NavPress, 2008), 31.

Chapter Seventeen

1. Ed Cheek, "Mickey Mantle: His Final Inning," American Tract Society, 2006.

Chapter Nineteen

1. William Peel and Walt Larimore, *Going Public with Your Faith: Becoming a Spiritual Influence at Work* (Grand Rapids: Zondervan, 2003), 182.

About EvanTell

EvanTell's mission is to declare the gospel, clearly and simply; to activate believers around the world; and to prepare the upcoming generations to reach the lost.

The ministry provides specialized training in evangelism for churches, colleges and seminaries, community outreaches such as pregnancy resource centers, disaster relief ministries, and in the workplace worldwide.

In 2012, EvanTell launched a four-session webinar that can be used to train and equip believers to share the gospel in the context of their life while at work. Believers may find it, along with other helpful training and tools for evangelism, at www.evantell.org.